Bob Wood

437 Old Trail

Balto. 12, Md.

THE ILLUSTRATED TRUE BOOK OF AMERICAN RAILROADS

THE ILLUSTRATED TRUE BOOK OF

AMERICAN RAILROADS

By ROBERT N. WEBB

GROSSET & DUNLAP · *Publishers* · NEW YORK

To

JOHN N. WEBB

We watched the 400's roll by

LIBRARY OF CONGRESS CATALOG CARD NO. 57-10567

PRINTED IN THE UNITED STATES OF AMERICA

CONTENTS

ACKNOWLEDGMENTS

The author wishes to acknowledge gratefully the assistance of the Association of American Railroads in helping him gather material for this book, and wishes also to express personal appreciation to Colonel Robert Selph Henry and Dr. Thomas J. Sinclair for their particular interest in the book. Others of the Association staff who read the galleys and offered their expert suggestions include Carlton J. Corliss, Donald M. Andersson, and Leonidas I. McDougle.

ILLUSTRATION AND PHOTO CREDITS AND SOURCES

The illustrations and photos on the following pages have been supplied by courtesy of the Association of American Railroads: 4, 9, 10 and 11, 17 (top), 21, 22, 24, 25 (bottom), 30 (top), 35, 39, 41, 46 (top and bottom), 51, 58 and 59, 62 and 63 (bottom), 69, 77 (bottom), 80, 82 and 83, 93, 95, 102 (bottom), 103, 109, 123 (bottom), 126.

The illustrations and photos on the following pages were obtained through Culver Service: v, 6, 8, 16, 18, 19, 20, 23 (top and bottom), 25 (top), 27, 30 (bottom), 33, 34, 38, 42 and 43, 48, 49, 50, 52, 53, 54, 57, 60, 61, 63 (upper right), 64, 65, 66, 67, 73, 74 and 75, 76, 77 (top), 78 (top), 79 (top), 81, 84, 85, 86 and 87, 88, 92, 94, 96, 97, 98, 99 (top and bottom), 139 (top and bottom), 140 (top and bottom), 141 (top and bottom), 142 (top and bottom), 143 (top and bottom), 147.

Other illustrations and photos are accredited as follows: pages ii and iii, *New York Central System;* pages 2, 5, 7, *Southern Pacific Railroad;* pages 10 and 11, *Union Pacific Railroad;* page 12, *New York Public Library;* page 13, *Southern Pacific Railroad;* pages 14, 15, 17 (bottom), *New York Public Library;* page 26, *Pennsylvania Railroad;* page 28, *Delaware & Hudson Railroad;* pages 29, 31, *Baltimore & Ohio Railroad;* pages 36 and 37, *Southern Railway Company;* page 40, *New York Central System;* pages 44 and 45, *Baltimore & Ohio Railroad;* page 47, *Reading Company;* page 55, *Library of Congress;* pages 62 and 63 (bottom), *Nashville, Chattanooga & St. Louis Railway;* page 68, *Library of Congress;* pages 70 and 71, *Pennsylvania Railroad;* page 72, *Norfolk & Western;* pages 78 and 79 (bottom), *Southern Pacific Railroad;* page 89 (left), *Union Pacific Railroad;* page 89 (right), *New York Public Library;* pages 90 and 91, *Union Pacific Railroad;* page 101, *New York Public Library;* page 102 (center), *by arrangement with Antonio Petruccelli, courtesy of Fortune Magazine, © 1938 by Time Inc.;* page 104, *New York Central System;* page 105, *New York Public Library;* page 106, *Fred Harvey;* page 107, *New York Public Library;* page 108, *Chicago, Rock Island & Pacific Railroad;* page 114, *New York Public Library;* page 117, *Union Pacific Railroad;* page 118 (top and bottom), *Southern Pacific Railroad;* pages 120 and 121, *Great Northern Railway;* page 123 (top and bottom), *Illinois Central Railroad;* pages 124 and 125, *Burlington Lines;* pages 128 and 129, *Santa Fe Railway;* page 131, *New York Central System;* pages 132 and 133, *Rock Island Lines;* pages 134 and 135, *The Milwaukee Road.*

THE ILLUSTRATED TRUE BOOK OF AMERICAN RAILROADS

CHAPTER I

LINKING THE CONTINENT

A BROAD, happy grin cracked the dried lips of the rider's dust-streaked face as he lashed his horse through the teeming work camp of the Central Pacific Railroad. Chinese laborers cried out as they leaped out of the path of this reckless rider with his hell-for-leather disregard for their safety.

In the center of the camp the rider reigned his horse to a plunging halt, jumped from its back and bounced over to a broad-backed Irishman in charge of a track-laying gang.

"Where's Stro, Mike?" he asked.

The Irishman nodded his head toward a boxcar on a siding about a hundred feet away.

"And where else but leavin' his palatial home right this minute and coming over this way to get the same news we're all awaiting for. Now be after telling me, your good friend, is it on or is it off? Come, lad . . ."

But the messenger spun around without replying, and strode off rapidly to meet the approaching figure. The two men each attracted a growing crowd as they closed the space separating them. By the time they met they were surrounded by a group of several hundred, all eager to hear the news.

The group, growing larger every second as men dropped their work and came trotting up, was gathered at the foot of Promontory Mountain in Utah. It was a warm morning late in April of the year 1869. These men were part of the work army of 15,000, which had pushed the rails of the Central Pacific eastward 700 miles from the coast of California,

BUILDING THE TRANSCONTINENTAL RAILROAD
Central Pacific forces building the western link of the first transcontinental railroad. Rail layers, shown in the foreground of the picture, were followed by gangs of Chinese laborers who spaced and spiked the rail to the ties.

True Book of American Railroads

and now were within twenty-five miles of joining track with the Union Pacific, which had pushed its twin ribbons of steel westward from the banks of the Missouri River at Omaha.

It would be only a matter of days until the continent of North America would be linked by rail. A dream of years would at last become a reality.

The messenger looked up into the heavily bearded face of James H. Strobridge, construction superintendent of the Central Pacific.

"The bet's on, Mr. Strobridge, sir."

The message spread rapidly through the crowd. The low, excited rumble which greeted it grew to a roar. Cheers went up, followed by still louder cheers. Shouts of "We can do it!" "We can beat 'em!" broke out everywhere.

Strobridge raised an arm.

"Back to your jobs," he ordered.

The crowd dissolved rapidly as Strobridge bored his way through it. There was never any holding back or lingering when Stro gave an order. As boss of all work crews of the Central Pacific, Strobridge held a firm grip on everyone of his 15,000 men. He seemed to be everywhere at all times along the road, driving his men, forcing his will upon them. He was ruthless in his treatment of any malingerer. He was particularly rough on the Chinese he was forced to accept. A tall, muscular man, given to profanity and violent tempers, he was seething inside as he strode back to his "palatial" home, the boxcar he lived in with his wife. He didn't share the enthusiasm of his men at the news "the bet is on."

For the past few weeks, Stro's men were mumbling in their dusty beards in angry disbelief at the track-laying record claimed by the Union Pacific. In one day, gangs under the Casement brothers, track-laying contractors for the Union Pacific, had laid eight and one half miles of track. This feat was startling indeed; in 1868, one to two miles per day had been the average. The record was just under six miles, set early in 1869 by Casement gangs. Now the U.P.'s gangs had outdone themselves.

The U.P. gangs boasted of their record. They loved to rub it in when chance meetings brought them together with any of the Central Pacific's crew.

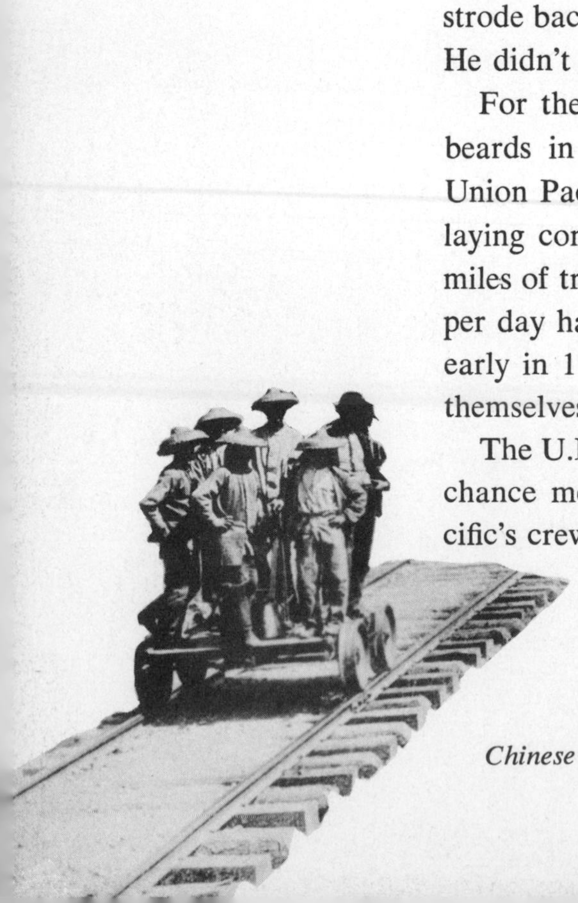

Chinese railroad laborers.

Charley Crocker—who with Leland Stanford, Collis P. Huntington, and Mark Hopkins had formed the Central Pacific—was as irked by the U.P.'s record as were his men. Crocker had resigned from the board of the Central Pacific to head up the construction company organized to build the Central Pacific. His pride was hurt. And T. C. Durant, vice-president of the Union Pacific, had offered to bet $10,000 the record could not be beaten.

A wily man, Charley Crocker. He bided his time. He had no intention of letting the U.P.'s record stand. And he wanted to win that bet.

First he sought out Strobridge.

"You heard what the U.P.'s done?"

Stro nodded his head.

"Over eight and a half miles of track put down in one day."

"A remarkable feat," replied Strobridge.

Crocker frowned. "Can you beat it?" he asked.

"I see no good to be accomplished in doing so."

"That's not the point. I ask if you can beat their record."

"The cost will be heavy," Strobridge said.

"Damn the cost. I want that record."

"We can beat them," Strobridge said quietly.

"Good. I want it done. I'll send word when I want you to start."

A construction camp of the Central Pacific Railroad in Utah, April, 1869.

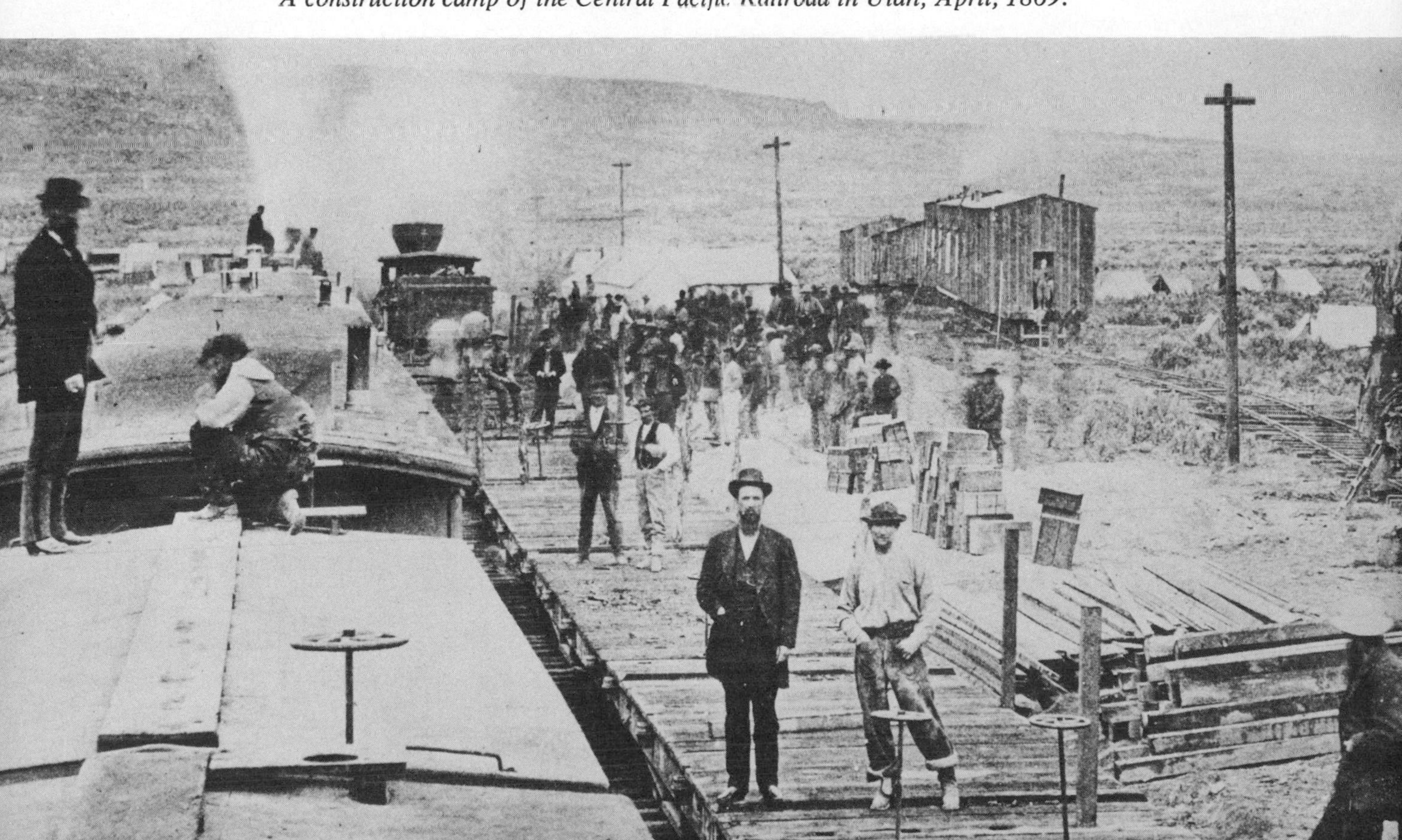

Crocker had reason to delay the start. He wanted to wait until the lines were so close together that there would be insufficient mileage left between the two roads for the U.P. to make a comeback if Strobridge broke the record.

On the day the messenger dashed into the Central Pacific's camp, only twenty-five miles separated the two lines, and this distance was growing shorter with each passing hour. Strobridge formed his plans. He would try for the record on the twenty-eighth of April.

Word of the impending attempt at breaking the track-laying record was flashed to every principal city in the United States, since the stringing of telegraph wires was done at the same time the track was laid. This message drove an already excited America to a point of frenzy. Everyone knew that it could only be a matter of days before construction of the first transcontinental railroad, started in the war year 1863, would reach its glorious, long-hoped-for completion.

At the opening of the year 1869, there was much speculation as to whether the lines would be joined in that year. As winter melted into spring, it became a certainty the lines would be joined. Excitement grew, tension mounted. Leading newspapers of all major cities sent special correspondents to the scene. Daily bulletins on progress were sent back. Boxes on page one of newspapers from Boston to Sacramento kept the records. Stories like the following were printed in every paper in the land.

"Three miles and 263 feet of track were laid by the Union Pacific today. The distance still separating the two railroads is now estimated to be less than 75 miles."

"The Central Pacific drove nearer its meeting with the Union Pacific today when track gangs working at a fever pace put down just twenty feet short of four miles of track. Track Boss Jim Strobridge estimates less than fifty miles now separates the two railroads."

Then came the story that the Union Pacific had laid eight and one half miles of track in one day. The nation went wild, only to grow even wilder when it learned the Central Pacific was out to crack that record.

The Central Pacific Sets a Record

On Tuesday, April 27th, Strobridge got everything in readiness. First he picked his men—eight sons of Erin—to handle the 600-pound

Chinese railroad laborers.

rails. Stro still didn't like the Chinese laborers, and, for such a task as this, he felt their slight bodies wouldn't be up to the grind. His Celtic octet included Pat Joyce, Tom Daily, George Wyatt, Ed Killeen, Fred McNamara, and three Mikes—Kennedy, Shay, and Sullivan.

Two miles of material—rails, ties, and spikes—were loaded on a train with a double-header—two engines—to push it. Stro wanted to gain every advantage he could. By having the engines push instead of pull the train, he could get his material nearer the last rail laid in the track by exactly the length of the two engines.

On the following morning, Wednesday, April 28th, all was set. Celebrities crowded either side of the grade. Charley Crocker chewed anxiously on his stogie. T. C. Durant stood aloofly a few paces apart. General Casement, whose two brothers were laying the Union Pacific's track, was there. So were engineers and surveyors of the U.P. to tape the mileage laid.

At exactly seven A.M., the whistle blew. The two engines gave a lurch. A sharp snap was heard over the engines' puffing. The train didn't budge.

Charley Crocker rushed over to Strobridge, who was on the cowcatcher of the first engine.

"What's happened? What's the matter?" he shouted.

Strobridge pointed. "Broke the push bar."

"Fix it, man! Fix it! We can't lose a second!"

Chinese laborers, working with pick and shovel, one-horse dump carts and black powder, carved a way through and over the granite Sierra Nevada mountains in California for the rails of the Central Pacific, from Sacramento to Promontory, a distance of 690 miles. There were no moderns implements in those days, not even scrapers for the grading.

Strobridge shook his head. "Can't be done. Take all day."

"You've got to! I tell you, you've got to!"

Stro was having trouble controlling his temper.

"Now just a dang minute, Charley. I'll get your record for you. But I'll do it my way. Now get off this engine and let me go to work."

"But when, man? When?"

"Tomorrow," was Stro's reply. "You'll have your record before sundown tomorrow."

Strobridge was as good as his word. He described the record setting himself to Robert Lardin Fulton, who recorded it word for word in his book *The Epic of the Overland*. These are Stro's own words:

"We waited a day and on Thursday, the 29th, I put the two engines in front to pull instead of push the train. With a will the men went to work, laying six miles in six hours and a quarter, two miles at a time. We changed horses every two and a half miles, but they were all tired and we gave them a good rest after that.

"We had kept them on the run, and at six o'clock we quit with a record of ten miles and two hundred feet. Every bolt was screwed up, every spike driven home so that we backed down over that sixty-foot grade at the rate of twenty-five miles an hour, twelve hundred men riding on the empty flat cars. Two Union Pacific engineers were there with their surveying chains, so there was no guess work and no contradictions. Our organization was as well drilled as any military company. Each rail was handled by eight men (The Irish Octet) four men on a side. They ran it out to the edge of the car, dropping it into place for the spikes to be driven, a man for each spike. When it was down, the men walked to the same spike on the next rail and drove it and on to the next all day. . . . There were men following up the trains, surfacing the track, filling in the dirt and making it ready for business. Nobody was crowded, nobody was hurt, nobody lost a minute."

When the track-laying gang, tired but triumphant, put down their tools at six o'clock, they had handled more than four million, three hundred thousand pounds of material in less than eleven hours—they'd taken a full hour out for lunch. In position had gone 25,800 ties; 3,520 six-hundred-pound rails had been secured by 55,000 spikes, 7,000 plates, and 14,000 bolts.

The Central Pacific employed over 10,000 Chinese laborers for the construction of the transcontinental railroad.

Charley Crocker took his $10,000 from Durant with a broad grin. No longer was there a ten-mile vacancy for unlaid rails—the two roads had come that close to a meeting point. The Central Pacific's record would stand. And stand it has, to this day—a world's record.

Linking the Continent

The nation's interest had been completely focused on the track-laying record. When it cleared its head from the celebration, it realized with a start that the great day it had been awaiting for so many years was at hand—less than ten miles now separated the track ends of the Central Pacific and those of the Union Pacific. The continent could be linked by rail on any given day.

Driving the Final Spike

Plans for laying the last rail and driving the last spike were formulated. The meeting place was to be at Promontory Point, Utah. This had been decided a month before, April 10th, by a joint resolution of the United States Senate and House of Representatives which provided: "That the common terminus of the Union Pacific and the Central Pacific railroads shall be at or near Ogden; and the Union Pacific Railroad Company shall build, and the Central Pacific Railroad Company pay for and own, the railroad for the terminus aforesaid to Promontory Point, at which place the rails shall meet and connect and form one continuous line."

The Union Pacific, charged by Congress with building the terminus, saw the last of its rowdy construction towns go up overnight at Promontory, including saloons, gambling dens, and noisy dance halls.

May 8th was the date set for the meeting of the rails and the ceremonies. But this date had to be changed to May 10th when the Union

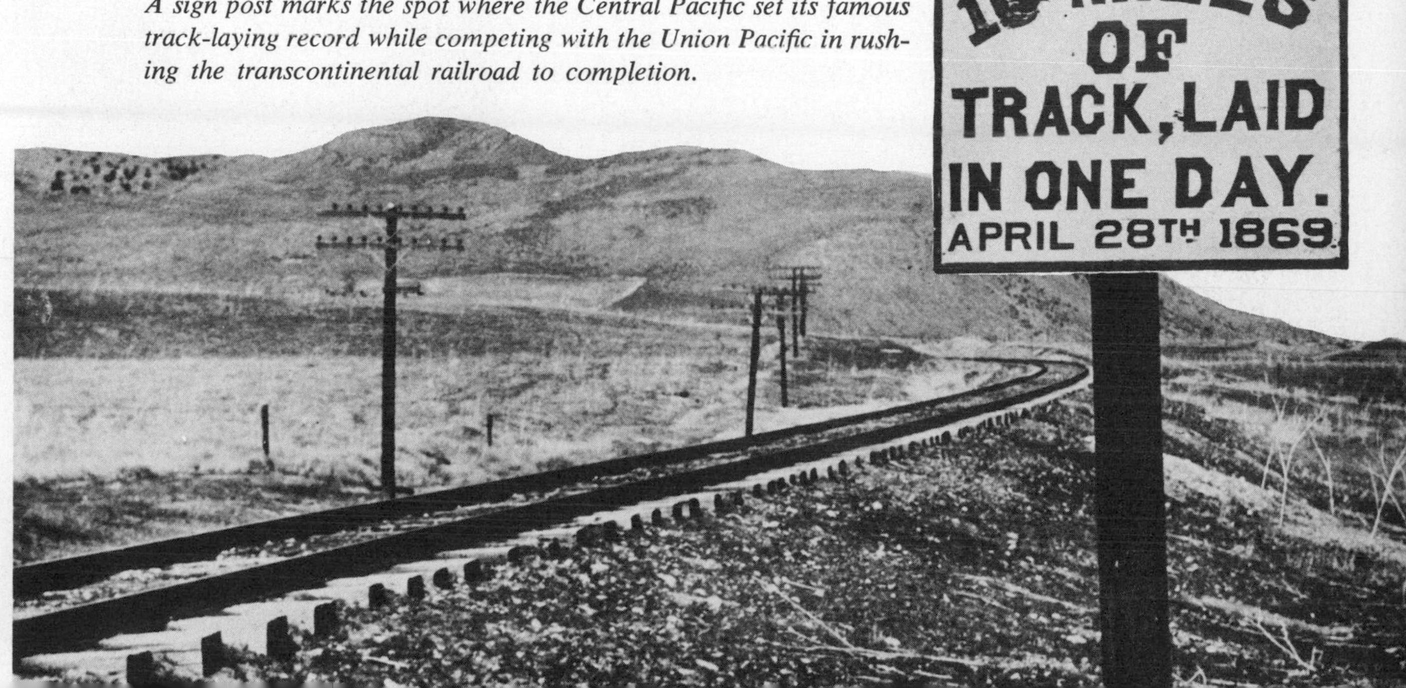
10 MILES
OF
TRACK, LAID
IN ONE DAY.
APRIL 28TH 1869

A sign post marks the spot where the Central Pacific set its famous track-laying record while competing with the Union Pacific in rushing the transcontinental railroad to completion.

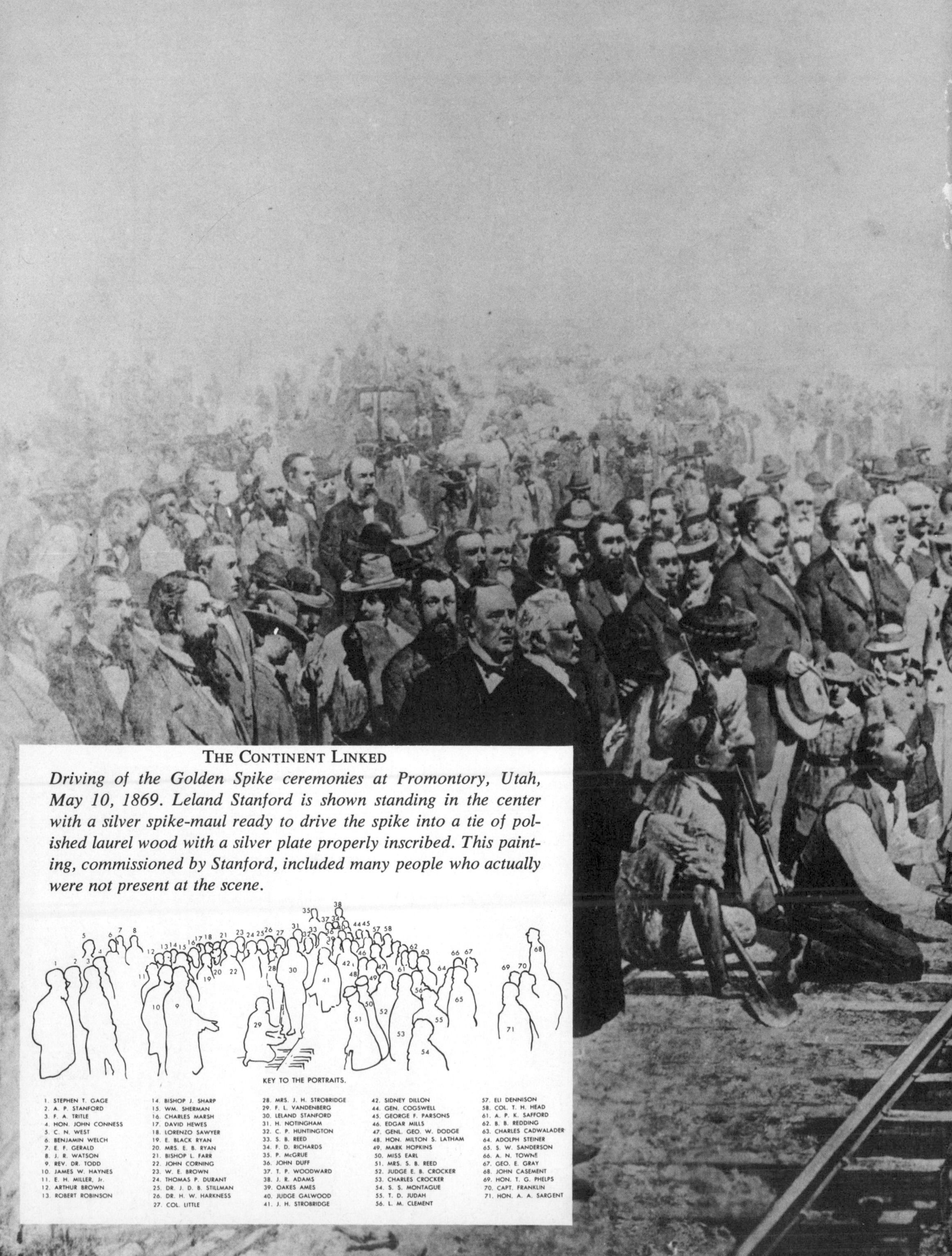

THE CONTINENT LINKED

Driving of the Golden Spike ceremonies at Promontory, Utah, May 10, 1869. Leland Stanford is shown standing in the center with a silver spike-maul ready to drive the spike into a tie of polished laurel wood with a silver plate properly inscribed. This painting, commissioned by Stanford, included many people who actually were not present at the scene.

KEY TO THE PORTRAITS.

1. STEPHEN T. GAGE
2. A. P. STANFORD
3. F. A. TRITLE
4. HON. JOHN CONNESS
5. C. N. WEST
6. BENJAMIN WELCH
7. E. F. GERALD
8. J. R. WATSON
9. REV. DR. TODD
10. JAMES W. HAYNES
11. E. H. MILLER, Jr.
12. ARTHUR BROWN
13. ROBERT ROBINSON
14. BISHOP J. SHARP
15. WM. SHERMAN
16. CHARLES MARSH
17. DAVID HEWES
18. LORENZO SAWYER
19. E. BLACK RYAN
20. MRS. E. B. RYAN
21. BISHOP L. FARR
22. JOHN CORNING
23. W. E. BROWN
24. THOMAS P. DURANT
25. DR. J. D. B. STILLMAN
26. DR. H. W. HARKNESS
27. COL. LITTLE
28. MRS. J. H. STROBRIDGE
29. F. L. VANDENBERG
30. LELAND STANFORD
31. H. NOTINGHAM
32. C. P. HUNTINGTON
33. S. B. REED
34. F. D. RICHARDS
35. P. McGRUE
36. JOHN DUFF
37. T. P. WOODWARD
38. J. R. ADAMS
39. OAKES AMES
40. JUDGE GALWOOD
41. J. H. STROBRIDGE
42. SIDNEY DILLON
44. GEN. COGSWELL
45. GEORGE F. PARSONS
46. EDGAR MILLS
47. GENL. GEO. W. DODGE
48. HON. MILTON S. LATHAM
49. MARK HOPKINS
50. MISS EARL
51. MRS. S. B. REED
52. JUDGE E. B. CROCKER
53. CHARLES CROCKER
54. S. S. MONTAGUE
55. T. D. JUDAH
56. L. M. CLEMENT
57. ELI DENNISON
58. COL. T. H. HEAD
61. A. P. K. SAFFORD
62. B. B. REDDING
63. CHARLES CADWALADER
64. ADOLPH STEINER
65. S. W. SANDERSON
66. A. N. TOWNE
67. GEO. E. GRAY
68. JOHN CASEMENT
69. HON. T. G. PHELPS
70. CAPT. FRANKLIN
71. HON. A. A. SARGENT

MAR 924

Pacific train carrying the official delegation, celebrities and additional newspapermen was late!

The weather on that morning of May 10th in 1869 was kindly. A gentle breeze stirred the grasses under the warming sun. The beginnings of a day which would go down in history were described by Sidney Dillon, a director of the Union Pacific, and later its president:

"The point of junction was the level circular valley about three miles in diameter surrounded by mountains. During all the morning hours the hurry and bustle of preparation went on. Two lengths of rail lay on the ground near the opening in the roadbed. At a little before eleven the Chinese laborers began leveling up the roadbed preparatory to placing the last ties in position. About a quarter after eleven the train from Sacramento with Governor Stanford and his party arrived and was greeted with cheers. In the enthusiasm of the occasion there were cheers for everybody, from the president of the Union Pacific to the day laborers on the road. The two engines moved nearer to each other and the crowd gathered around the open spaces. Then all fell back a little so that the view should be unobstructed."

This was the moment the nation was waiting for. Celebrations had been arranged in every major city in the country. The telegraph company had set up lines to Washington, New Orleans, Chicago, Philadelphia, Boston, New York, Omaha, and San Francisco. Bells in each city were to be rung by the strokes of the hammer, wired to telegraph instruments, as it drove the last spike.

Leland Stanford, former governor of California and president of the Central Pacific, and T. C. Durant, vice-president of the Union Pacific, were to strike alternate blows on the final spike. Other dignitaries and celebrities gathered around these two men. The crowd—composed of Chinese, Irish, Mexicans, Negroes, and Indians—edged nearer.

Strobridge and Reed, construction boss of the U.P., dropped the last tie, made of California laurel, into place. The tie was polished until it glistened and had imbedded in it a silver plaque reading: "The last tie laid on the completion of the Pacific Railroad, May 1869."

Silence was called for as Stanford took his place on the north side of the rail, Durant on the south side. Stanford picked up a silver maul. He was handed the golden spike.

CENTRAL PACIFIC RAILROAD.

No. 1, TIME CARD No. 1.

To take effect Monday June 6th, 1864, at 5 A. M.

TRAINS EASTWARD.						TRAINS WESTWARD.		
Frt and Pass No 3	Frt and Pass No 2	Pass & Mail No 1.		STATIONS.		Frt and Pass No 1	Pass & Mail No 2.	Frt and Pass No 3.
5 P M leave	1 P M leave	6.15 A M, L	......	Sacramento.	......	8.45 A M arr	12 M arr.	6.40 P M ar.
5.50 } 5.55 } mt frt	2.15	3.55	18	Junction.	18	3	11.20	5.55 } 5.50 } mt. Ft
6.09	2.38	7.05	22	Rocklin.	4	7.40	11.07	5.37
6.22	2.55	7.15 meet F.	25	Pino.	3	7.15 mt pass	10.56	5.25
6.40	3.30 P M arr	7.30 A M arr	31	Newcastle.	6	3.45 A M, L	10.30 A M, L	5 P M, L

Trains No. 2 and 3 east, and 1 and 3 west, daily, except Sunday.
Trains No. 1 east and 2 west, daily.

LELAND STANFORD, President.

So. Pacific Rlr.

The Central Pacific Railroad's first timetable issued June 6, 1864.

Linking the Continent

Now the stillness which had come over the gathering was broken only by the clattering of the telegraph instruments. The first message went out:

> "ALMOST READY. HATS OFF. PRAYER IS BEING OFFERED."
>
> "WE HAVE GOT DONE PRAYING. THE SPIKE IS ABOUT TO BE PRESENTED."
>
> The east wired back:
>
> "WE UNDERSTAND. ALL READY IN THE EAST."
>
> "ALL READY NOW. THE SPIKE WILL SOON BE DRIVEN. THE SIGNAL WILL BE THREE DOTS FOR THE COMMENCEMENT OF THE BLOWS."

Stanford raised the silver maul over his head, brought it down and . . . missed! Howls of delight went up from the laborers. Stanford swung again, and this time hit the spike. He handed the maul to Durant. To the great delight of the crowd, Durant missed his first swing, too. But then the spike was sunk into the laurel tie and the telegrapher at 12:45 P.M. tapped out the four letter word:

"DONE."

That one word set off a nation-wide frenzy of joy. President Grant received the message in the White House. In Philadelphia, the Liberty Bell rang out from Independence Hall. In New York a 100-gun salute was fired, and in famous Trinity Church the *Te Deum* was sung. San Francisco began a celebration which lasted two days.

The engineers nudged the throttles of their engines, and the Central Pacific's wood burner "Jupiter" and the Union Pacific's coal burner No. 119 inched forward over the last two rails until their cow-catchers touched.

The nation was joined by two bands of iron.

LAST SPIKE
COMPLETING FIRST
TRANSCONTINENTAL
RAILROAD
DRIVEN AT THIS POINT
MAY 10TH 1869

This is the monument which now marks the spot where the first transcontinental rails were joined on May 10, 1869. The "last spike" was unspiked on September 8, 1942, when the rails were taken up and track materials salvaged for the war effort. The monument stands far from a railway today in a lonely place, north of the Great Salt Lake, across which the main line now stretches by trestle and fill at considerable saving in distance and grade compared with the original route.

Recently the Interior Department announced plans to transform this spot into a Golden Spike National Historical Site.

CHAPTER II

HORSEBACK AND STAGECOACH

THE NATION was now linked from coast to coast by twin rails of iron, the golden spike symbolic of the giant strides the young country had made in solving its transportation problems. American travelers had come a long, long way from that first landfall of the *Mayflower* at Provincetown. They had come on their own sturdy legs, by dugout canoe and pirogue, by horseback, pillion, coach and prairie schooner—by any means at hand, slowly but certainly, discarding the old way for the newer, the faster.

Just two months less than forty-one years had passed from that July 4th, in 1828, when Charles Carroll, the last survivor of those who had signed the Declaration of Independence, tossed the first spadeful of dirt marking the beginnings of the Baltimore & Ohio Railroad. This venerable gentleman, in his ninetieth year, said on the occasion: "I consider this among the most important acts of my life; second only to the signing of the Declaration of Independence, if even it be second to that."

Little wonder young America was jubilant. Not only had the War between the States come to an end, but with the driving of the golden spike on May 10, 1869, there came a strong feeling of unity. The nation was joined.

There came to the nation, too, a great feeling of relief. No longer would travelers have to depend on the stagecoach, or the prairie schooner—time-consuming, uncomfortable, uncertain. Yet what would this nation have done without the stagecoach, without the horse, with

its ever restless citizens who "don't always know where they're going but they're on their way?"

Horseback and Stagecoach

In this nation's early days, the fastest and most comfortable means of travel was by water. This was fine, of course, for persons wishing to go from one place to another along the eastern seaboard. But for the American pioneer, with his urge to go west, the horse and the "trodden paths" were his best means of getting from one community to another.

Wise early settlers took their travel ways from the Indian. They followed the paths marked by Indian migration, paths that wound through thick forest underbrush. These paths were widened and deepened by the heavy boots of the colonists and the hoofs of their cattle. At first, the paths, never more than twelve to eighteen inches in width, led short distances, as groups of families broke from the original settlements and ventured farther on. New colonies were being settled to the south and to the west. They opened chances for trade. The paths began to lengthen, and to widen.

Actually, the nation's first roads were officially called "trodden paths," as ancient court records of New England show. Many of the routes of these twelve-inch "trodden paths" are today the right-of-ways of our railroads, or of our express highways.

If it is true, as often said, that modern Americans never walk when they can ride, they certainly came by it naturally. Many years were to pass in early colonial days before horses were plentiful enough, and of good enough breed, for our early settlers to be able to give up walking from town to town, colony to colony. In the South, travel by horseback was even more necessary than it was in the North. Southern settlers did not live in closely knit communities as they did in New England. They lived on widely separated plantations of vast acreage.

When horses were still scarce, a system of "riding and tying" was developed. When two persons started out on a journey with but one horse, one of them would ride the horse ahead to a designated spot, tie the animal, and proceed on foot. As the horse rested, the second traveler would eventually reach the spot, mount and ride until he overtook his companion. The companion would then mount, ride ahead and tie. This procedure continued until the two men and their one horse reached their destination.

As the early years rolled by, the trodden paths widened to permit the passage of the chaise, the carriage, and the coach. Use of these horse-drawn vehicles, however, was largely confined to towns and cities, because roads away from inhabited places were nearly impassable. One horseback traveler in the 1820's described a road in these picture-creating words: "If the mud does not get quite over your boot-tops when you sit in the saddle, they call it a middling good road."

Since roads were so bad, and city streets but little better, the coach was slow in development. Only a dozen or so coaches were to be found in the cities of Philadelphia, New York, and Boston in the early 1700's. In Puritan Boston, the use of a coach was considered worldly to the point of sinfulness, and for many years coach travel was strictly banned on the Sabbath. Josiah Quincy related an anecdote pointing up the strictness with which this law was enforced. A young carriage driver who was dashing through the town of Andover one Sabbath was halted and threatened with arrest by an outraged church deacon. The young man put on his saddest face and told the deacon, "Tell the good people of Andover that you permitted me to pass because my mother is lying dead in Boston." The deacon released his grasp on the horse's reins and permitted the young man to proceed. As the young man surged forward in a cloud of dust, he shouted back to the deacon, "You may also add, if you please, that she has been lying dead there for some twenty years."

The Stagecoach Rules Supreme

By 1800, and for the next three decades, the stagecoach ruled supreme as the method of travel. Stagecoach lines extended all over the country, and the operation of a line was usually a flourishing business.

An American stagecoach such as was used between New York and Philadelphia about 1790.

Horseback and Stagecoach

The stagecoach in those days was as important to the nation's economy and its development as are the railroad and airline of today.

Despite poor, uncomfortable equipment, and roads which were no more than widened, mud-filled "trodden paths," travelers of those days made few complaints. They cooperated with the stagecoach driver to the point of helping him lift his coach out of a quagmire, muddying up their clothes in so doing, and often getting out and walking to rest the horses. They also cooperated with the driver in his efforts to keep the coach from overturning. A foreign traveler in America wrote of a stagecoach trip he took: "The driver frequently had to call to the passengers in the stage to lean out of the carriage, first on one side, then on the other, to prevent it from oversetting in the deep ruts with which the road abounds. 'Now, gentlemen, to the right!' Upon which the passengers stretched their bodies halfway out of the carriage to balance on that side. 'Now, gentlemen, to the left!' "

The first Boston & Providence railroad cars were stagecoaches with flanged wheels, not too different in appearance from the stagecoaches that traveled over the dirt highways of America.

One of the earliest, and most famous, of the stagecoach lines was that running between Boston and Providence. Boston travelers took the stagecoach to Providence, and there continued their journey to New York by boat. The fare was three dollars, but competition became so fierce among rival stagecoach lines that the fare dropped until competing companies eliminated *all* charge, and even offered passengers a bottle of wine and a free dinner just to get them to ride their respective lines. For over a week, while this early "price war" was under way, travel between Boston and Providence reached new highs. Each company tried to outdo the other in the vintage of the wine offered and the succulence of the dinner. One Boston dancing master, a favorite among the social set, dismissed his classes and shut down his academy for a week. He did nothing but travel back and forth from Boston to Providence, and so satisfied his urge for the changing scene, good wine and food absolutely free.

As rival stagecoach companies sought to improve their service and shorten the time required to travel from one city to another, roads came in for increased attention. The first of the nation's turnpikes was started at Alexandria, Virginia, and stretched west to the lower Shenandoah. Today the word "turnpike" has come to mean the highway itself. Its original meaning was quite different. The turnpike was a long sapling or staff which was placed across the early roads to halt the traveler until he had paid his toll. Once the money was paid for using the road, the pike was turned aside and the journey could be continued. The turnpike was actually the tollgate. Passengers were required to pay their toll each time they came to a "turnpike," although stagecoach operators paid their tolls annually.

Of the early roads built, the most important was the National Road, so named because it was built by the federal government. It extended westward from Cumberland to Wheeling, one hundred and thirty miles, and cost $1,750,000. It was considered the finest road ever built, sixty feet wide, constructed of stone broken to pass through a three-inch ring. This stone was then covered with gravel and rolled with a heavy iron roller. Of this road it was written: "That great contractor, Mordecai Cochran, with his immortal Irish brigade—a thousand strong, with their carts, wheelbarrows, picks, shovels, and blasting-tools—graded the commons and climbed the mountain side, leaving behind them a roadway fit for an emperor."

In his history of the National Road, Thomas B. Searight said traffic was so heavy that "it looked more like a leading avenue of a great city than a road through rural districts. . . . Excitement followed in the wake of the coaches all along the road. Their arrival in the towns was the leading event of each day, and they were so regular in transit that farmers along the road knew the exact hour of their coming without the aid of watch or clock. They ran night and day alike. Relays of fresh horses were placed at intervals of twelve miles as nearly as practicable. . . . Teams were changed almost in the twinkling of an eye. The coach was driven rapidly to the station where a fresh team stood ready harnessed waiting on the roadside. The moment the team came to a halt, the driver threw down the reins, and almost instantly the incoming team

The "General Wayne" Inn of Baltimore in pre-railroad America. A favorite stopover for travelers.

was detached, a fresh one attached, the reins thrown back to the driver, who did not leave his seat, and away again went the coach at full speed."

Horseback and Stagecoach

Even at fullest speed, stagecoach travel left much to be desired. As late as 1826, the trip by stagecoach from Boston to New York took over a week. Josiah Quincy, then president of Harvard College, described a trip he took to New York that year: "I set out from Boston in the line of stages of an enterprising Yankee, Pease, by name; considered a method of transportation of wonderful expedition. The journey to New York took up a week. The carriages were old and shackling, and much of the harness of ropes. We reached our resting place for the night, if no accident intervened, at 10 o'clock, and, after a frugal supper, went to bed with a notice that we should be called at three, which generally proved to be half-past two, and then, whether it snowed or rained, the traveler must rise and make ready, by the help of a horn lantern and a farthing candle, and proceed on his way over bad roads, sometimes getting out to help the coachman lift the coach out of a quagmire or rut, and arrived in New York after a week's hard traveling, wondering at the ease, as well as the expedition, with which our journey was effected."

Six years later the same trip was made in forty-one hours, but passengers were not allowed to stop at night even for the shortest of sleeps, but rode straight through, night and day. The fare was eleven dollars.

When Quincy's stagecoach stopped for the night, the distinguished president of Harvard might have been confronted with the following set of rules from an old way-stop:

RULES OF THIS TAVERN

Four pence a night for Bed
Sixpence with Supper
No more than five to sleep in one bed
No boots to be worn in bed
Organ grinders to sleep in the Wash house
No dogs allowed upstairs
No Beer allowed in the Kitchen
No Razor Grinders or Tinkers taken in

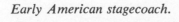

Early American stagecoach.

Fares charged stagecoach passengers depended not only on the length of the trip, but on competition, the comfort or lack of it of the coach itself, and on the weight of the passenger. Early stagecoach lines in Indiana and Illinois set the weight of each passenger at one hundred pounds. That weight required one fare. If the passenger weighed one hundred and fifty pounds, he was charged one and a half fares, and if he were such a trencherman as to weigh two hundred pounds, then he paid two fares.

The stagecoach driver was a man of considerable importance. His position was the same as that of today's captain of an ocean liner. His word was law. His favor was sought. He was on first-name terms with the great of the land. A nineteenth-century writer, recalling his boyhood, wrote the following about two stage drivers named Mills and Howell: "My earliest recollections are intimately associated with coaches, teams and drivers, and like most boys raised in an old stage tavern, I longed to be a man, when I could aspire to the greatness and dignity of a professional stage driver. In my boyish eyes no position in life had so many attractions as that of driving a stage team. A Judge, a Congressman, even Henry Clay or President Jackson did not measure up to the character of John Mills or Charley Howell in my juvenile fancy."

Rich in color and lore that have outlived the memories of its wearying discomforts, the stagecoach clattered into history with the rise of the railroad. But not until the proprietor of a stage operating swiftly between New York and Philadelphia had been touched with prophecy. He named his coach "the flying machine."

The village inn was also the travel depot of the early American rural community.

CHAPTER III

THE FIRST TRAINS

"WHAT can be more palpably absurd and ridiculous than the prospect held out of locomotives traveling twice as fast as stagecoaches!"

These words, appearing in the *Quarterly Review* of London in 1825, summarized public opinion in England regarding the future of travel by railroad. This feeling prevailed despite the facts that England had been using some form of railed-track transportation for nearly two hundred years, that it had had steam locomotives for twenty-one years, and iron rails for nearly one hundred years. Wheeled vehicles on rails, drawn by horses, had been used in Newcastle, England, as early as 1630.

Much this same feeling was to be found in America at this time. Yet America, within a few years, was to take a giant step and quickly draw abreast of railroad development in England, despite that nation's two-hundred year head start, then forge ahead of Great Britain.

For a locomotive to exceed the speed of a stagecoach—much less to double it—was considered sheer insanity on both sides of the Atlantic. In America, speeds being attained by stagecoaches were thought to have reached their limit, and this limit was considered nothing short of miraculous.

A trip from Washington to Baltimore—thirty-eight miles—in a regular stagecoach drawn by three horses took a day and a half, although the faster mail coaches over the same road made the trip in eighteen hours. This was in 1812, and by 1822, the trip from Providence to Boston—43 miles—had really been speeded up. As one letter writer described the trip. "We were rattled from Providence to Boston in four

The Granite Railway, the first method of railroad transportation in America, as seen in a woodcut made in 1830.

hours and fifty minutes. If anyone wants to go faster he may send to Kentucky and charter a streak of lightning."

Only a few visionaries disagreed with this opinion, and they quickly became cautious in their public utterances, if they didn't want to be called lunatics. After stating that it would be absurd for anyone to think a locomotive could go twice as fast as a stagecoach, the *Quarterly Review* continued: "We should as soon expect the people of Woolwich to suffer themselves to be fired off upon one of Congreve's ricochet rockets as trust themselves to the mercy of such a machine going at such a rate. . . . We trust Parliament will, in all railways it may sanction, limit the speed to eight or nine miles an hour, which we entirely agree . . . is as great as can be ventured on with safety."

Thomas Tredgold, author of an early book on English railroads, wrote in 1825: "Locomotives must always be objectionable on a railroad for general use, where it is attempted to give them a considerable degree of speed. . . . That any general system of carrying passengers would answer, to go at a velocity exceeding ten miles an hour, or thereabouts, is extremely improbable."

Another writer on the same question, Nicholas Wood, put these words down in 1825: "It is far from my wish to promulgate to the world that the ridiculous expectations, or rather professions, of the enthusiastic

An experimental railway and locomotive was built by Colonel John Stevens at Hoboken in 1825 to prove the practicability of railroading. It was the first steam locomotive to run on track in America.

speculation will be realized, and that we shall see engines traveling at the rate of twelve, sixteen, eighteen or even twenty miles an hour. Nothing could do more harm toward their general adoption and improvement than the promulgation of such nonsense."

These gentlemen were all for horses, and felt sure that the horse would forever furnish a train's motive power.

GEORGE STEPHENSON, INVENTOR

Richard Trevithick didn't think so. Neither did George Stephenson. Both were Englishmen. Both were dedicated to the development of steam locomotion. By many, Trevithick is considered the father of railroading. On the other hand, there are those who insist that Stephenson is the father of the locomotive, even though Trevithick as early as 1797 developed a three-wheeled steam-powered vehicle, seventeen years before Stephenson constructed his first practical locomotive. However, it was Stephenson who brought the locomotive to its highest point of development in the first three decades of the 1800's.

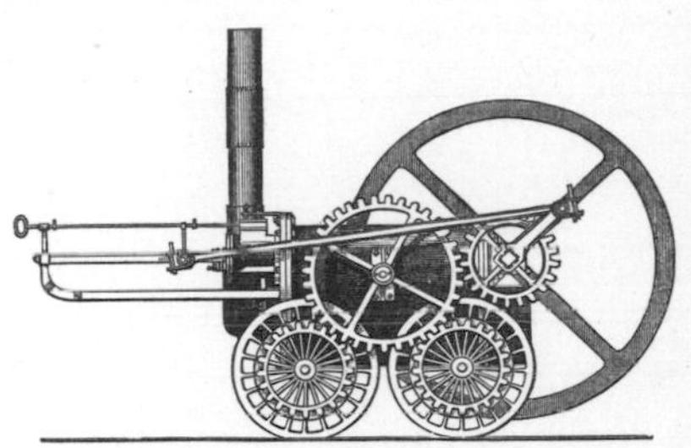

Trevithick's Tram-Road Locomotive, 1804.

With his cousin and partner, Trevithick built two more steam locomotives, and in 1805 built an engine known both as the Trevithick Newcastle steam engine and the Gateshead locomotive. Actual tests were made with this locomotive on a strap railroad. There are no records of what these tests proved, nor of what significance they had in the future development of railroading.

Stephenson, in 1814, drew keen attention to his first locomotive. In that year he built a steam engine which pulled eight loaded coal cars over a tramway at four miles an hour. This feat was significant to English coal miners, with their ever-pressing need for cheap, effective coal-mine transportation. This engine was called the *Blucher* and preceded by fifteen years his more famous locomotive, the *Rocket*.

However, the skeptics still far outnumbered the visionaries. As late as 1825, Stephenson was forced to curb his beliefs when the proposed Liverpool and Manchester Railway asked Parliament for a franchise. Called before the Parliamentary committee considering the franchise

Horse car of 1829, the first means of transportation on the Baltimore & Ohio Railroad.

application, Stephenson was taken aside by the railroad's lawyer, William Brougham, and told that if he even mentioned the possibility of any such speed as twenty miles per hour, he would "inevitably damn the whole thing, and be himself regarded as a maniac fit for Bedlam." Stephenson heeded this advice and held his speed forecasting down to twelve miles per hour. Even so, the committee denied the application, mumbling to one another about Stephenson's sanity.

Four years earlier, though, Stephenson had been of assistance in the passage of the Stockton and Darlington Railway Act. However, when this road was opened to traffic, horses furnished the motive power. On downgrades, the horses were led up on a platform built at one end of a passenger car, and enjoyed the downhill ride with their more human but equally frightened fellow passengers.

On this same railroad, and in the same year 1825 when Stephenson met Parliamentary defeat, he was also to conduct a test which changed the minds of doubting Thomases on both sides of the Atlantic. His newest engine, the *Locomotion,* made a public trial pulling twenty-nine cars plus tender at an average of eight miles an hour. The total load was ninety tons. Word of this feat swept throughout England, and became even more outstanding when it was compared to the operation of the Surrey Iron Railway, where teams of horses pulled fifty-five ton loads at an average of three miles per hour.

No longer was Stephenson considered a "maniac fit for Bedlam." When construction of the Liverpool and Manchester Railway was begun, its franchise finally granted in 1827, Stephenson was named its supervisor. On completion of the road, he induced the company's officers to put up a prize of $2,500 for a locomotive that could pull three times its weight at a speed of ten miles an hour. Then he built a locomotive and won the prize himself.

The locomotive was the famous *Rocket*. At the historic Rainhill trials of 1829, the *Rocket,* weighing four tons, pulled a fourteen-ton load at a speed of twenty-nine and a half miles per hour.

There is no record of what the Parliamentary committee thought when it learned of this accomplishment, but, in America, Senator Oliver H. Smith of Indiana took the floor to proclaim: "I tell you that in England they have already run railroads fully loaded at thirty miles per

The "Blucher," first steam locomotive built by the celebrated English engineer, George Stephenson, in 1814.

hour and they will yet be run at higher speeds in America."

This statement was not to go unchallenged, as are few statements in the U. S. Senate. An opponent arose and cried out: "Either you are crazy or you think we are fools, for a man *could not live at that speed!*"

The First Trains

Although America lagged behind England in the earlier development of steam-powered land vehicles, the younger nation did have a crude form of tracked transportation as early as 1764. A cable-operated tramway of grooved logs was constructed at a military camp at Lewiston, New York. It was used to haul supplies from the lower Niagara River to the top of a 300-foot bluff.

Another early cable-operated tramway was that constructed in 1800 on Beacon Hill in Boston. It had a wooden track, and was used in leveling off the top of artist John S. Copley's estate. The earth removed from the top of the hill was carried down by gravity cable and used as fill.

GEORGE STEPHENSON

Other such tramways were built to connect rock quarries with boat landings. The most famous of these early wooden railways was the Granite Railway, in Quincy, Massachusetts, over which granite blocks were hauled to build the Bunker Hill monument. The road was about three miles long, running from the quarry in Quincy to a wharf on the Neponset River. The track was capped with strap iron fixed to oak facing atop pine logs which were set on stone ties. Horses were used to pull the four cars comprising the road's rolling stock. On completion of the road, proud Bostonians boasted of the "first railroad in the United States."

This claim did not go undisputed. It was pointed out a few years later that the Granite Railway had never operated a passenger service. One "first" of dubious distinction was set by the road. Several years after the road had been in operation, four visitors from Boston were given permission to ride in an empty car. As the car was being hauled up the quarry, a rope broke, the car plunged to the bottom, seriously injuring three of the passengers and killing the fourth, who thus became America's first railroad fatality.

The first locomotive to be built in America was the somewhat-addled brainchild of Oliver Evans, Philadelphia blacksmith, boat builder and steam-engine enthusiast. In 1804, he was commissioned to build a

The four-ton "Rocket," built by George Stephenson, received the award in the Liverpool and Manchester Railway competition held in England, October 6, 1829. Conspicuous in yellow and black with a tall white chimney, it drew ten tons at a rate of ten miles an hour on its first test, an astounding feat for that time.

dredge. A dredge he built, but he added a steam engine not only to operate the dredging machinery, but added wheels and a propeller to the dredge, turning out what was to be the world's first amphibious craft. It was called the *Orukter Amphibolos*. Unfortunately, as Evans started his combination locomotive-steamboat-dredge across the rutted streets of Philadelphia toward the Schuylkill River, the wheels and axles collapsed. In defending his beliefs as to the future of steam-powered travel, though, Evans foresaw the day of the streamliner. He prophesied that to reduce air resistance so as to attain such speeds as twenty miles per hour, "the body of the carriages will be shaped like a swift swimming fish to pass easily through the air."

Other locomotives were built by American inventors and engineers. The foremost among them was John Stevens, who for years had tried with no great success to stimulate interest and raise funds to build railroads in New York and New Jersey. Stevens built the first steam engine in America to run on a railed track. However, this track was a small circular one laid out in the backyard of his home in Hoboken,

Model of John Stevens' experimental locomotive built in 1825.

New Jersey. His engine could reach a speed of twelve miles per hour with six passengers. Its only true claim to a place in American railroad history rests with the trial runs it made and the interest it aroused among the curious and the doubters.

The Stourbridge Lion

One person interested in Stevens backyard railroad was John Jervis, chief engineer of the Delaware and Hudson Canal Company. This firm operated a series of inclined, gravity railroads between its coal mines at Carbondale and its canal terminus in Honesdale, Pennsylvania, a distance of about sixteen miles. Jervis felt that efficiency might be increased and costs decreased by the use of steam locomotives on the line, so in 1828 he sent his assistant, Horatio B. Allen, to England to purchase four locomotives. Among the four was the *Stourbridge Lion,* the first steam locomotive to run over a commercial railroad track in the New World. The *Lion's* trial run—its first and only trip—was a shattering performance in more ways than one.

The nine miles of the track which stretched between the two termini were on trestles made of hemlock. Just outside of Honesdale where the trial run was to be made the first trestle spanned Lackawaxen Creek at a height of thirty feet. Many of the trestle's timbers had warped under the blazing summer sunshine, and it didn't take too much of a breeze to start the trestle swaying. It was over this bridge that Engineer Allen was to run the *Lion,* which weighed nearly eight tons, although on its purchase it was thought to weigh nearer three.

It was to be a gala day in Honesdale. Crowds gathered from miles around. A cannon had been borrowed for the occasion, and its resounding boom was to start the *Lion* on its way. By mid-morning of Saturday, August 8, 1829, the curious lined the track. The *Lion* puffed and snorted as pressure built up in its boiler. It presented a truly awesome sight, with its boldly painted red-and-gold lion's head on the front of the boiler.

Engineer Allen, a daring man, mounted the cab. His hands reached for the control. If he heard the spectators' comments that the *Lion* would never make it over the trestle, he gave no evidence of it. On the contrary, he had decided that if he was going to make it over the trestle,

Oliver Evans' "Orukter Amphibolos."

the faster the better, and had decided to give the locomotive full throttle.

The cannon boomed. Allen jerked on the throttle, and with a squeech of spinning wheels, smoke belching from the stack, the *Lion* was off. So intent was Allen on the trestle ahead, he didn't see the cannon, overcharged with powder, explode, tearing the arm off of Alva Adams, the man who touched it off. The *Lion* rocketed along the three hundred feet of track before it hit the trestle. It hit that shaky and wobbling bridge at its full speed—twenty miles per hour. The trestle swayed. Allen caught a quick glimpse of the waters thirty feet below, and then he was safely across. He continued for another three miles, reversed his engine and came puffing back to his starting point. The *Lion* had done it!

It was to be its only trip, though. Immediately it was decided that the *Lion* was much too heavy. Its day of glory was over. The *Lion* was placed in a shanty alongside the track, where souvenir hunters stripped it to the boiler, which was left to rust. What remains of the *Stourbridge Lion*—the boiler, some wheel tires, and a walking beam—can now be seen at the Smithsonian Institution in Washington.

The "Stourbridge Lion," purchased in England for the Delaware & Hudson Railroad Company, introduced practical steam locomotives to America when Horatio Allen drove this engine three miles on August 8, 1829, at Honesdale, Pennsylvania.

The First Trains

The Tom Thumb

Of all the early locomotives built in America, none was to achieve more lasting fame than the *Tom Thumb*. This locomotive, named for its size—or, rather, lack of it—not only pushed the car which carried the first American passengers to be transported by steam power, but it engaged in the first race with a horse-drawn car on rails.

The *Tom Thumb* came into being for two reasons, the one leading to the other. When the Baltimore and Ohio Railroad was planned, it was believed that the road would have to be operated with horse-drawn vehicles. This was the English influence. Because of the many curves on the road, British engineers stated that it would be impossible to employ steam power. They said no locomotive could pull a train around a curve of less than a 950 foot radius. On the B. & O.'s first thirteen miles of track between Baltimore and Ellicott's Mills, there was one abrupt curve of 150 foot radius. No British locomotive could possibly negotiate this curve.

A spirited race between Peter Cooper's engine, the "Tom Thumb," and one of the early horse-drawn cars used on the Baltimore & Ohio Railroad took place on August 25, 1830, between Relay and Baltimore, Maryland.

Officials of the B. & O., however, realized if they were ever to extend their road to the Ohio Valley, horse-drawn trains would never furnish sufficient power, nor speed. During their deliberations on the problem, with stockholders surrendering their stocks believing the venture would end up in failure, Peter Cooper came to the rescue. Cooper had ample reason to be concerned. He had purchased three thousand acres of land in Baltimore along the right of way of the B. & O., and if the road was not going to be commercially feasible, then his land investment would be worthless.

PETER COOPER

Cooper described the situation to the *Boston Herald* as follows: "The directors (of the B. & O.) had a fit of the blues. I had naturally a knack of contriving, and I told the directors I believed I could knock together a locomotive that would get around that curve. . . .

"So I came to New York and got a little bit of an engine, about one-horse power (three and one-half inch cylinder and fourteen-inch stroke), and carried it back to Baltimore."

Next Cooper got a small boiler, about as big as a wash boiler, hooked it up to his small engine, and set the result up on a four-wheeled flat car. It worked. On August 28, 1830, the *Tom Thumb,* itself host to five passengers and the engineer, and with thirty-six passengers on the flat car, made the thirteen-mile run to Ellicott's Mills in one hour and twelve minutes, and returned in fifty-seven minutes.

Even though this was an outstanding first in American railroad history, newspapers of the day made little of it. One New York daily considered the achievement of so little importance that it didn't carry the story of the event until a month after it took place and then buried it in fourteen lines, without a headline, at the bottom of a column on its second page.

A trial between the "Tom Thumb" and one of Stockton's and Stokes' Horse Cars.

But if newspapers and the general public displayed a lack of interest, stagecoach proprietors in Baltimore were greatly alarmed. They saw a real threat to their thriving business. The largest of these stagecoach firms was Stockton and Stokes. Within a few days of the *Tom Thumb's* first trip, they hurled a challenge. Their offer was to race a horse-drawn car against the *Tom Thumb*. Cooper accepted the challenge.

A double track had been laid between Baltimore and Ellicott's Mills. The *Tom Thumb,* with as many passengers as could crowd aboard, made the run from Baltimore to the end of the line. There, awaiting the start of the race, was the horse-drawn car. No fools the managers of Stockton and Stokes! They had selected their finest charger to carry their banner. The horse was a magnificent grey, described as "of great beauty and power."

Cheers and cries of defiance by the rivals in the two cars shook the air at the word "Go!" The grey leapt forward under the lash of its driver's whip, and was off to a fast start, quickly setting up a lead of

The "Tom Thumb" was a one-horsepower experimental engine mounted on a car frame and geared to an axle. The boiler tubes were made from musket barrels, and its one cylinder was only 3½ inches in diameter.

a quarter of a mile. The *Tom Thumb* could only gather speed slowly, since its blower—to give the engine forced draft—was operated by a belt attached to an axle. The faster the axle revolved, the greater the forced air from the blower, the hotter the fire, the greater the steam pressure. Slowly the *Tom Thumb* gained on the grey. Then it overtook the horse-drawn car, and taunts and cheers arose from those aboard the steam-operated train. The grey's driver lashed the horse to even greater effort, and for a few moments the horse kept abreast. Then the *Tom Thumb* pulled away, and soon was far in front of its rival. But, with victory in sight, the blower belt broke, and steam pressure went down. Despite Engineer Cooper's efforts to replace the belt with the car in motion—he severely lacerated his hands in the process—the *Tom Thumb* kept going slower and slower, until the horse-drawn car came thundering past to win the race.

Despite the shouts of superiority sent up by adherents of horse-drawn trains, the *Tom Thumb* settled once and for all the type of motive power which was to move the B. & O. Locomotives had arrived. Cooper's land investment was saved.

CHAPTER IV

EARLY AMERICAN RAILROADS

BEFORE the *Tom Thumb* demonstrated conclusively that the steam locomotive was the answer to the search for power needed to move America's trains, many other forms of propulsion were tested. Looking back on them today, they seem utterly ridiculous—some of them so fantastic that one might be excused if he wondered why such tests and trial runs were even attempted. However, as ludicrous as many of these methods of motive power may seem to us today, they all made a contribution, no matter how slight, to the rapid progress which ended in America's having the finest system of railroads the world has ever known. The well-known trial-and-error system never found a better field for exploration than in the beginnings of America's railroads.

A noted German engineer, Chevalier von Gerstner, expressed this feeling most precisely when he was asked why he had come to America to study railroad development instead of England, which at that time was ahead of the New World in railroading:

"That is the very thing I want to escape from," he said, "this system of England, where George Stephenson's thumb, impressed upon the plan, is an imprimatur which gives it currency and makes it authority throughout Great Britain; while here, in America, no one man's imprimatur is better than another's. Each is trying to surpass his neighbor. There is rivalry here out of which grows improvement. In England it is imitation—in America it is invention."

But even Chevalier von Gerstner might have been forgiven a bewildered chuckle or two had he been along the B. & O.'s right of way

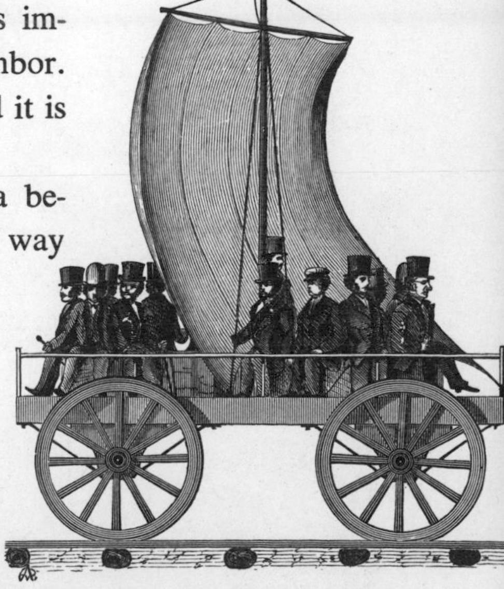

Sail Car as it appeared with a party of excursionists on the South Carolina Railroad, March 19, 1830.

not too many months before the *Tom Thumb* made its historic run. He would have seen a bowl-shaped basket breezing down the rails under full sail. The wicker basket, holding a half-dozen passengers, was set upon a small flat car, about the size of today's hand-car. A tall mast reached skyward, and from it billowing in the wind was a sail. It was a sailing car, built by a Baltimorean named Evan Thomas and named the *Aeolus*. The car went merrily along until the wind died down, then rolled to a lazy stop. A few minutes later the wind came up again, but came from the opposite direction, and the passengers found themselves being blown right back to their starting point.

Sail was not the answer.

Soon after this experiment, another was tried on the B. & O. This was a horse-operated locomotive. But the horse didn't pull the train. The horse was placed upon a car fitted with a treadmill, and as it patiently trod this moving platform, power was transmitted to the car's wheels and the train moved ahead. Great enthusiasm greeted this contrivance. Prominent citizens of Baltimore, newspaper editors, and other celebrities were invited for a trial run. The guests were seated on benches surrounding the horse, and at the word "giddyap," off they went. All went well for a mile or two. Then an inquisitive cow came up to take a look, decided she didn't approve, hooked her horns into one of the wheels, and sent the car, passengers, horse and all careening off the track on its side.

Comment in the Baltimore papers the following day was unfavorable, to put it mildly, and this form of power was abandoned.

The Best Friend of Charleston

Further south, residents of Charleston, South Carolina, had no intention of lettting the B. & O. help build Baltimore into the largest seaport on the Atlantic. They envisioned a railroad which would tap the fast-growing inland areas, and thus bring Charleston to full economic tide and make it a thriving seaport to rival any other.

A bill granting a charter for a railroad between Charleston and Hamburg became law in December, 1827, and by January of 1830 six miles of the road had been laid. Various means of power were tested on this road, as they

The "Flying Dutchman," a horse-operated locomotive, was another experiment of the South Carolina Railroad.

had on the B. & O., even including a sailing car. This sail car proved no better than the *Aeolus*. Its mast, sail and rigging blew overboard as the car reached a speed of twelve miles per hour, carrying most of its fifteen passengers with it.

Horatio Allen, the intrepid engineer of the *Stourbridge Lion*, had been summoned to Charleston late in 1829 to take charge of building the road. Firmly convinced that steam was certain to be the future means of power, he gained permission from the management to commission the West Point Foundry of New York City to build the road two locomotives. Thus, the South Carolina Canal and Railroad Company became the first American railroad built expressly for steam locomotion. It was also to become the first railroad in this country to operate a regularly scheduled passenger service.

In October, 1830, the first of the two locomotives arrived in Charleston aboard the steam packet *Niagara*. No inanimate object ever received a wilder, more enthusiastic reception. Charlestonians immediately envisioned a rebirth of trade. They felt sure they would regain the cotton business which had shifted to Savannah, Georgia. So, they named the little engine *The Best Friend of Charleston.*

In test runs, *The Best Friend* more than lived up to its name mechanically. One specification made in ordering the engine was that it must make a speed of ten miles an hour. In a test, traveling alone, it made as high as thirty miles an hour, and, pulling four cars containing fifty passengers, it made a run at twenty-one miles per hour.

Christmas 1830 was a gala day in Charleston. *The Best Friend of Charleston* was going to make its first formal run. From all over South Carolina people flocked to the seaport city. Bands played. Fireworks were shot off. *The Best Friend* was hooked up to a three-car train. On a flat car immediately behind the engine rode a detail of U. S. Army artillery men. A small cannon had been borrowed from the government to lend its resounding boom to the significant occasion. Behind the flat car were two carriages, resembling covered wagons with high sideboards. In these rode officialdom, the socially distinguished, and other celebrities of the day. Around one o'clock, one of the soldiers pulled the lanyard of the cannon, and, with the resulting boom, *The Best Friend*

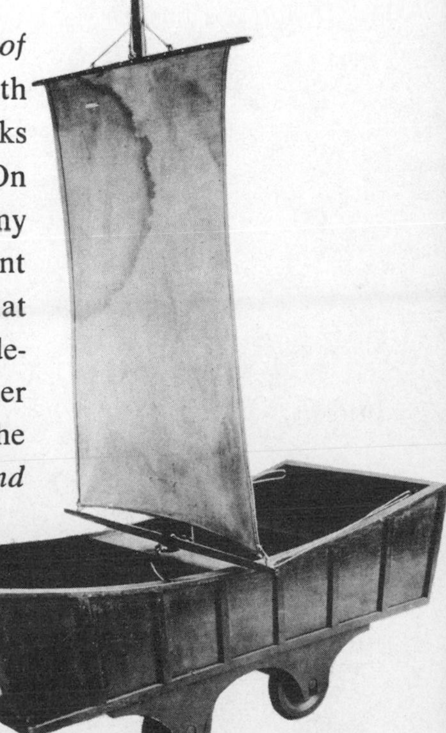

Even though the builders of the South Carolina Canal and Railroad Company had already decided on steam engines as the motive power for the railroad, they built experimental cars such as this one powered by a huge sail. Such experiments, however, served only to confirm the previous decision to use steam engines.

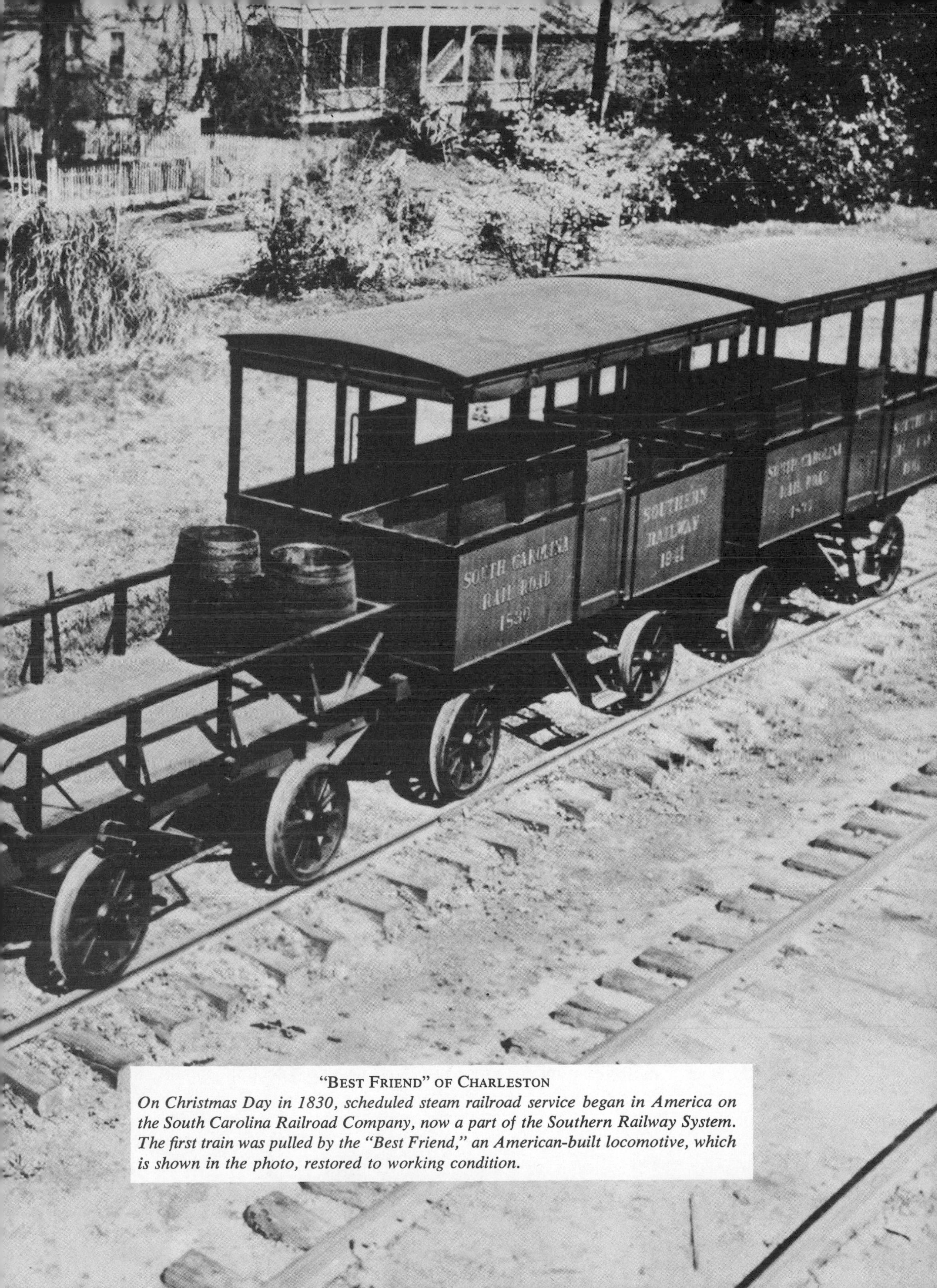

"BEST FRIEND" OF CHARLESTON

On Christmas Day in 1830, scheduled steam railroad service began in America on the South Carolina Railroad Company, now a part of the Southern Railway System. The first train was pulled by the "Best Friend," an American-built locomotive, which is shown in the photo, restored to working condition.

puffed out of Charleston. One passenger described the ride: "Away we flew on the wings of the wind at the speed of fifteen to twenty-five miles an hour, annihilating time and space, and leaving all the world behind. . . . The engine darted forth like a live rocket, scattering sparks and flames on either side, passed over three salt water creeks hop step and jump, and reached the end of the line before any of us had time to determine whether or not it was prudent to be scared."

In less than three years, the South Carolina Canal and Railroad Company had pushed its track to Hamburg, a distance of one hundred and thirty-six miles, and proudly announced itself as the longest railroad in America, which it was. As early as 1831 the same road transported several sacks of mail and became the first railroad to carry the U. S. mail.

Still another first can be chalked up to the South Carolina Railroad, one which saw the end of *The Best Friend*. The Negro fireman on the locomotive got more and more annoyed at the hissing sound of steam

The "Best Friend" was built at the West Point Foundry Shops in New York City for the South Carolina Railroad, arrived by ship at Charleston on October 23, 1830, and after several trials in November and December, made its first excursion trip, as shown, on Saturday, January 15, 1831.

escaping from the safety valve. He figured he could fix that. He shoved the safety lever down, effectively shutting off the escaping steam, and to hold the lever in place, he sat on it. Not for long. The little engine's boiler shortly exploded, sending the fireman to heaven, both literally and figuratively, for it was the first fatality on a steam locomotive.

The explosion caused much concern among officials of the railroad, as well as among prospective passengers. To eliminate this danger, a flat car was placed right behind the engine and loaded with bales of cotton, reaching as high as the roofs of the coaches behind it. If another boiler was to explode, the flying metal would be caught by the bales of cotton, not by the passengers. Apparently no one gave any thought to what might happen to the engineer and fireman if such an unhappy event was to take place again.

Right after this, Manager Horatio Allen installed another invention on his train. A flat car with a thick coating of sand was placed in front of the new engine, the *West Point*. On this car was built a blazing bonfire of pine knots—the first headlight. Night travel by train came into being.

THE DEWITT CLINTON

During the early stages of the Baltimore and Ohio and the South Carolina Canal and Railroad Company (soon shortened to the Charleston and Hamburg), the north was not sitting idly by, watching developments. In New York State, a charter had been given the Mohawk and

The locomotive "West Point" operated on the South Carolina Railroad in 1831. The car with bales of cotton strapped on it was known as a "barrier car" and was run with every passenger train as a means of protecting passengers from steam or hot water in case an accident should occur.

Hudson Railroad for a road between Albany and Schenectady, a distance of seventeen miles. This was in 1826, a year before the South Carolina road came into existence. By August 1831 all rails had been laid between the two thriving New York towns.

From the same West Point Foundry which built *The Best Friend,* the Mohawk and Hudson had ordered a locomotive. This was the now-famous *DeWitt Clinton,* twelve feet in length, with four forty-eight-inch wooden, iron-capped driving wheels, and weighing 6,758 pounds. After some test runs, this twelve-foot, fire-eating iron horse was pronounced ready to go into service. Everyone in Albany was on hand that hot August morning in 1831—members of the legislature, leading citizens, drummers. Stretching out from Albany all the way to Schenectady, lining the right of way, were farmers with their families decked out in their Sunday best, sitting in wagons and carriages. The horses hitched to these vehicles calmly munched grass, grateful for a day off from heavier work. Their calmness was to be of short duration.

The *DeWitt Clinton* was backed up and hooked onto its train. Right behind it was a small flat car with two barrels of water and a pile of wood. The water was hooked up to the engine's boiler by a leather hose. Behind this forerunner of the coal car were hooked three passenger cars, looking exactly like what they were, stagecoach bodies on flanged wheels. Each coach had seating room for six, but so mad was the scramble to take a ride on this first steam train that additional passengers clambered aboard the roofs of the coaches. Behind the passenger cars were six more flat cars with wooden benches for seating. Every seat was taken within minutes after the cry went up for all to get aboard.

The "DeWitt Clinton," first locomotive and train of passenger cars to be run in New York State. It was ordered from the West Point Foundry by John B. Jervis, chief engineer of the Mohawk & Hudson Railroad, and was the third locomotive built in America for actual service on a railroad.

John T. Clark, probably the first conductor in America, went up and down the train, with the call which has come down through railroad history, "Tickets, please." Retracing his steps, Clark climbed aboard the "coal car," took out a long tin horn, and gave a mighty blast. Engineer Dave Matthews, who had built the engine, gave a yank on the throttle, and the *DeWitt Clinton* leaped forward to its task. Each car behind the engine gave a similar leap, but not at the same time. Three-foot iron chains connected each car with the one behind it. The slack snapped taut by the lurch of the engine. Conductor Clark would have gone sprawling overside had he not quickly grasped a roof support and held on for dear life. In turn, each car behind sprang forth with a similar jerk. Passengers inside the coaches fared far better than those on top, several of whom were tossed to the ground. But those on the wooden benches on the six rear flat cars fared the worst. As each car snapped into action, the benches went over backward, depositing the passengers on the floor and in each other's laps. Once the train stretched out, the going was smooth, and shouts of approval went up. But not for long.

As the *DeWitt Clinton* gathered speed, the smoke and blazing sparks from the engine's pine-pitch fuel flattened out, forming a long black cloud of smoke and hurling embers directly on the ten-car train. Again, the passengers in the coaches had the better of it. Although blinded by smoke, not as many burning embers settled inside the coaches as came to rest among those on the open flat cars. Back at the rear of the train, passengers were soon flailing away at their own and other's bodies in an attempt to put out the fire of their burning clothes. Those who had umbrellas raised them to fend off the falling sparks, but soon the umbrellas caught fire and were hastily jettisoned. After only a few miles the whole train was composed of volunteer firemen, fighting a moving conflagration. Along the route sightseers were thrown into confusion: their horses reared and ran away, and the spectators screamed.

Fortunately, the *DeWitt Clinton* was nearing its first watering stop. Engineer Davis applied his brakes—only the engine had them—and they worked. The *DeWitt* came to a plunging halt, and a reverse replica of the train's start took place. Passengers were plunged forward this time, as each car jounced to a stop, blockaded by the car in front of it.

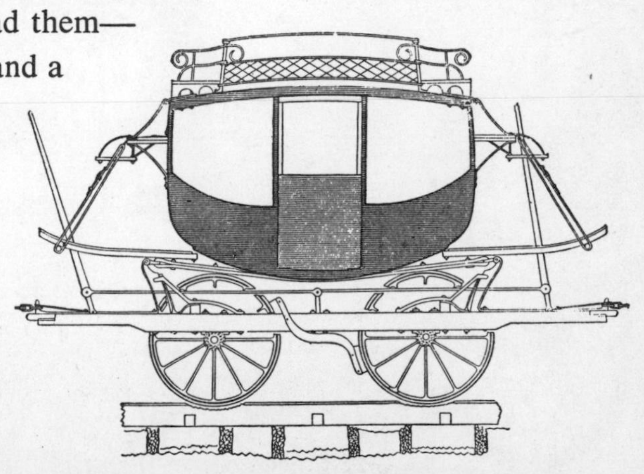

From this drawing were constructed the railway coaches which were pulled by the locomotive "DeWitt Clinton" in 1831. These early railroad coaches were little more than stagecoaches with flanged wheels and coupling devices.

The first thing the passengers did when they tumbled from the cars was rush to the water and finally extinguish their burning clothes. Next they tore down the rails of a farmer's wooden fence, cut them into correct lengths, and wedged them between each car comprising the train. When the *DeWitt Clinton* started up for the remainder of its run, the fence rails held firm, and the train moved off with only gentle lurching. The rest of the trip brought no new adventures. True, smoke and blazing embers continued to rain down on the unprotected heads of the passengers, but by this time their clothes had become so badly damaged that they didn't care. Not a single passenger abandoned the ride—pioneer bravery indeed.

All along the way, of course, horses, cows, and oxen reared, snorted, bellowed, and took off fast at the approach of this burning dragon, which belched smoke and flame from its head.

In Schenectady, a royal welcome was given the *DeWitt Clinton* and its courageous passengers. After due time had been given for the in-

An early view of Boston as seen from the southwest near

spection of both, the train started back for Albany. On its return trip, not a single animal was seen along the right of way.

For the record, the trip up had taken forty-six minutes. The trip back was made in thirty-eight minutes, the last six miles taking only fourteen minutes.

This road was the beginning of the great railroad which gave America its most famous train—the *Twentieth Century Limited.* This was the first link of what was to become the New York Central twenty-two years later. Ten more roads were granted charters and built before there was a continuous line from Albany to Buffalo on the Great Lakes. At first, each of these lines operated independently, with no regard for the schedules of the connecting road. Passengers on one line would disembark upon reaching its end, climb aboard a car of the next line in the chain, and then wait until this train elected to move on. Often these delays between trains were as long as a full day. Dissatisfaction among passengers grew until finally the eleven separate railroads which oper-

the intersection of the old Providence & Worcester Railroad.

ated on the tracks stretching from Albany to Buffalo were united to form the New York Central.

Building the Pennsylvania Railroad

Foremost in the minds of Eastern railroad builders was the desire to push their track westward to tap the fast-growing commerce of those states and territories of the Ohio river valley and beyond. Unlike the builders of the Charleston and Hamburg, whose track ran across flat country, Eastern builders were faced with a terrain which threw up a formidable barrier to their progress. The Adirondacks and the Catskills barred the path in New York. New England was confronted with the

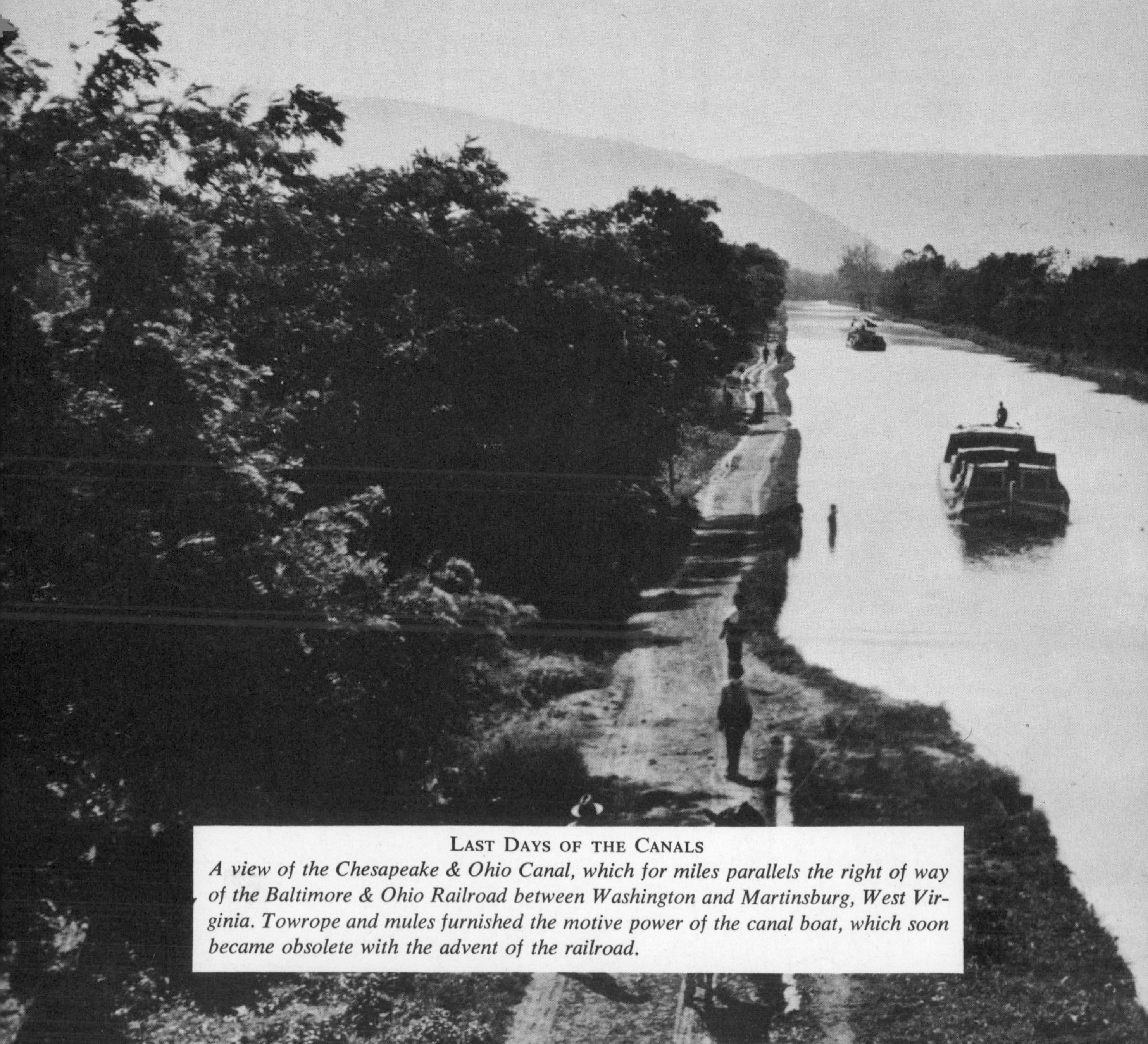

Last Days of the Canals

A view of the Chesapeake & Ohio Canal, which for miles parallels the right of way of the Baltimore & Ohio Railroad between Washington and Martinsburg, West Virginia. Towrope and mules furnished the motive power of the canal boat, which soon became obsolete with the advent of the railroad.

Berkshires and the White Mountains; the south, of course, had the Appalachian Range rising between it and the Mississippi Valley. In Pennsylvania, the Alleghenies stood between Philadelphia and Pittsburgh.

In Philadelphia, as elsewhere throughout the nation, interest in railroads was at a fever pitch. Out of this public enthusiasm came the start of the great locomotive works which was to build the nation's horses of iron for years. It all started with a man named Franklin Peale, the proprietor of the Philadelphia Museum. Then, even as now, there were those who saw profit to themselves in capitalizing on the public's curiosity. Peale wanted a steam locomotive for his museum. He turned to a jeweler named Matthias Baldwin. Baldwin, an expert watch re-

pairer, had broadened his business activities to the manufacture of machinery for printing calico and making bookbinders' tools. In the process, he had built a stationary steam engine. Peale reasoned, if Baldwin could make a stationary steam engine, why not one which moved under its own power? He approached Baldwin, and Baldwin built a model locomotive which could pull four small cars. This train was installed in the museum and people flocked to ride it. The tiny engine and its four cars created more public interest than did Independence Hall and the Liberty Bell.

From this model, Baldwin went on to build *Old Ironsides* at the request of the founders of the Philadelphia, Germantown and Norristown railroad. *Old Ironsides* wasn't much of a success in its early trials, but this was true of almost all American-built engines in early days, since the builders had little or no experience in their new work. However, Baldwin finally worked out most of the quirks in his locomotive, and it went into operation in November of 1832. Local newspapers hailed the little engine as the "wonder of the day." On one trial, with many stops for repairs, she did as much as a mile in one hour. A year later, as Baldwin further improved the little engine, she made the truly remarkable speed of one mile in fifty-eight seconds, running alone.

MATTHIAS W. BALDWIN

In actual operating service between Philadelphia and Norristown, *Old Ironsides* apparently didn't like to go out in the rain. The company advertised its schedule as follows: "The locomotive by M. W. Baldwin, of this city, will depart daily when the weather is fair, with a train of passengers. On rainy days, horses will be attached."

Although Baldwin publicly announced that he would build no more locomotives after *Old Ironsides,* orders came in so rapidly that the jeweler was forced to put aside his watch-repairing tools, and pick up the heavier ones which were to build the great Baldwin Locomotive Works.

"Old Ironsides." The wheels were made with heavy cast-iron hubs, wooden spokes and rims, and wrought-iron tires. The tender was a four-wheeled platform, with wooden sides and back, carrying an iron box for a water tank, enclosed in a wooden casing, and with a space for fuel in front.

Early American Railroads

While most Philadelphians were cheering the feats of *Old Ironsides* or taking time out to plank down their pennies for a ride on the model train in the Philadelphia Museum, another group was viewing with considerable alarm the two-armed threat to their city's financial position. On the south, the B. & O. was pushing its roadbed across the mountains of West Virginia to the Ohio Valley, with the announced intention of reaching Pittsburgh. On the north, the Erie Canal was carrying more and more cargo back and forth from the West to the northern seaboard.

Philadelphia capitalists decided in 1845 that it was high time the Pioneer Fast Line between their city and Pittsburgh be improved upon. The Pioneer Fast Line had been in operation between Pennsylvania's two largest cities since 1834. The Fast Line proudly claimed that the trip could be made in four days, and perhaps it was once or twice, but more often the trip took twice that number of days. Even so, this was much faster than the twenty days it took by stagecoach. In those days passengers from Philadelphia to Pittsburgh made the trip in several stages.

"Old Ironsides" is shown leaving the old depot at Ninth and Green Streets, Philadelphia, Pa. Regular passenger service began on November 26, 1832, when the locomotive with six cars filled with passengers left Philadelphia for Germantown.

They started out in horse-drawn cars for the first two miles of their trip. At this point the horses were unhitched and the cars attached to a cable to haul them up a two thousand eight hundred-foot inclined road to the top of a one hundred and eighty-seven-foot hill. They were towed by nine-inch-thick hawsers, some a mile in length, which cost $3,200 each. The hawsers were wound up on drums operated by 60-horse-power stationary engines.

Once atop this hill, the cars were coupled to a steam locomotive for the ride to the end of the line at Columbia. At Columbia the cars were loaded on canal boats for the one hundred and seventy-two-mile trip to Hollidaysburg. At Hollidaysburg the cars returned once again to rails for the most unusual part of the entire trip. Here the traveler was confronted with a thirty-six-mile trip to Johnstown over the crest of the Allegheny Mountains at a height of two thousand five hundred feet. For this rise, and descent, of twenty-five hundred feet in thirty-six miles, a series of inclined planes was built, operated by stationary engines, again reeling up the heavy hawsers which pulled the cars. This was the famous Allegheny Portage Railroad.

At Johnstown, it was back to water for the passengers for the remaining 104-mile leg to Pittsburgh on canal boats.

By 1846 there was no longer any question in the minds of Philadelphia financiers that Baltimore was becoming a serious rival due to the commerce the B. & O. was creating. In that year the Pennsylvania Railroad was incorporated. Under the brilliant direction of J. Edgar Thomson, the Pennsylvania bought up the Philadelphia and Columbia Railroad, the Allegheny Portage, put down new road beds and track, and, in July, 1858, the first through train ran from Philadelphia to Pittsburgh without having to transfer passengers.

Thomson became president of the Pennsylvania in 1852 and guided the road's destinies until 1874. He is considered one of the greatest operating railroad men this nation ever produced.

The Pennsylvania Railroad crossing the Alleghanies via inclined planes between Harrisburg and Pittsburgh.

CHAPTER V

WAR RIDES THE RAILS

AMERICAN railroad growth in the three decades from 1830 to 1860 was truly amazing. Lines were extended to the eastern banks of the Mississippi River, and plans were being discussed to push rails across the deserts and the mountains to the Pacific Coast. New England, a slow starter in the railroad race, was now interlaced with several roads. The South and Middle Atlantic States were criss-crossed with a network of interlocking lines offering passengers transportation to even the remotest of points, and by 1860 there were already 2,175 miles of railroads west of the Mississippi.

In all, over 28,000 miles of track had been spiked down in the area of the United States east of the Mississippi River by the outbreak of the Civil War. Then, for four years, the laying of new track came to a standstill as Northerner fought his Southern brother. In 1856, over 3,600 miles of railroad were built; only 700 miles of track were laid down in 1865. Destruction of railroads during the war years was tremendous. Both sides captured roads, destroyed them or used them, battled for them many times, rebuilt them, only to have them again captured and destroyed. The Southern railroads suffered the greatest destruction, and at war's end, but a fraction of the South's pre-war 10,000 miles of track was still in place.

But, although these were years of violent destruction, of damage in unreckoned millions, they were also years in which some of the greatest feats of daring occurred on America's railroads. There was the winning of a battle by a single locomotive's whistle. There were Morgan's raids; Stonewall Jackson captured rolling stock for the Southern cause

through trickery; Northern spies stole the Southern engine, *The General*. Possession of the B. & O. changed from Confederate troops to Union troops frequently.

NORFOLK CAPTURED BY A WHISTLE

Most unusual of all these deeds of daring, perhaps, was the strategy employed by William Mahone, president of the Norfolk and Petersburg Railroad, now the Norfolk and Western, in capturing the navy yards at Norfolk, held through the first years of the war by Union troops. The Commandant of the Navy Yard, although called upon many times to surrender, had repeatedly refused, knowing that the

A United States Military Railroad engine down the "Banks," near Brandy, Virginia, in April 1864.

Southern forces barely outnumbered his own. He was waiting for help to come by sea from the North. At the same time, the rumor was strong that the Confederate garrison in Norfolk was soon to be reinforced by troops coming from Georgia and the Carolinas.

Word reached Mahone that Union gunboats had arrived and were steaming up the James River to destroy the railroad's drawbridges. Quickly assembling a brigade of soldiers, President Mahone piled them aboard flat cars and moved out to defend his railroad. Much to their welcome surprise, no gunboats were found in the vicinity of any of the bridges or anywhere else on the James. Mahone ordered his engineer to reverse the train and head back for Norfolk. On the way, he had a brilliant idea. He knew that the Union troops in the Navy Yard were expecting the rebel reinforcements, so why not let them think they had arrived? As the train drew near Norfolk, President Mahone had his engineer blast out with his whistle at irregularly spaced intervals. The engineer was really an artist with his whistle, even able to change its pitch by regulating the amount of steam he fed into it. The engine's bell clanged in accompaniment to the many-toned, irregularly blown whistle, so that not only did the embattled Union troops believe several trains of reinforcements from the South had arrived, but citizens of Norfolk thought so, too, and rushed into the streets to welcome them. That night, the Union garrison slipped out of the Navy Yard in the dark and headed north, blown there by the whistle of a single locomotive.

Morgan's Raiders

It was Christmas night of 1862. Snow flurries covered most of Kentucky. Union troops stationed in stockades at either end of the bridges on the Louisville and Nashville Railroad had relaxed after the extra rations given them for their Christmas supper and were dreaming dreams of Christmas at home. Those dreams were rudely shattered at dawn the next morning as the Confederate General John H. Morgan unleashed the first of his lightning swift raids which were to put the L. & N. Railroad out of operation for six months.

He struck first at Upton, sixty miles south of Louisville, capturing the telegraph office. By a series of misleading telegrams to the Union

General Sherman's men wrecking a railroad on their march to the sea in 1861.

General Boyle in Louisville, Morgan got all the information he needed, and completely fooled Boyle as to his whereabouts. With 4,000 mounted troops, he struck bridge after bridge along the line, successfully routing the Union troops and destroying bridges and trestles. The stockades he overran were not easy to take. They were of heavy log construction, two stories high, well stocked, with a lookout tower giving excellent observation in all directions. Raider Morgan toppled them over, knocked out of commission the road which was to be used by

Raider Morgan's freebooters entering Washington, Ohio. As shown by an illustration which appeared in Harper's Weekly, *August 15, 1863.*

Northern troops for penetration into Georgia, and captured 1,900 prisoners. Only General Sherman in his march through Georgia matched the railroad destruction of this daring Southern raider.

Stonewall Jackson's Coup

At the outbreak of the war, the South was hard pressed for rolling stock, particularly locomotives, since all engines at that time were built in the North. Stonewall Jackson was quick to appreciate the vital part railroads would play in the war, and devised a plan to stock up on rolling stock. General Jackson was encamped at Harper's Ferry with his army. He dispatched an aide to John W. Garrett, president of the B. & O., with the complaint that night coal trains, eastward bound through Harper's Ferry, made so much noise his men couldn't sleep. He asked that these trains be scheduled to pass the encampment between the hours of 11 A.M. and 1 P.M. President Garrett acceded to the request. A few days later the aide again stood before President Garrett, this time with the complaint that the empty coal cars rumbling westward at night disturbed his men just as much. Couldn't the empties be dispatched so as to pass through Harper's Ferry westbound during the same two hours the loaded cars were heading east? Again President Garrett complied. Harper's Ferry for two hours daily became the busiest railroad center in America.

Stonewall Jackson was now ready for his coup. He dispatched a force of men to Martinsburg in West Virginia. Starting at eleven o'clock the next morning, this force was to allow all eastbound trains through until 12 noon. Then stop all traffic both ways. A second force carried out the same orders on the Maryland side of the Potomac River, and Stonewall Jackson had all trains trapped in a distance of less than thirty miles. He then rerouted these trains on a branch line which ran into Winchester, Virginia, Southern-held territory, and the South, for a time, was well stocked with engines, freight and passenger cars.

The B. & O.'s War Troubles

This ruse of Stonewall Jackson was but one of an extended series of raids, and track destruction which plagued the B. & O. throughout the Civil War, making that road one of the most fought-over railroads in

Troops tearing up a railway.

history. For the B. & O. the War between the States began some eighteen months before those fatal shots were fired at Fort Sumter, South Carolina. This road's introduction to the conflict came on October 17, 1859, when the fanatical John Brown and his small band of rabid followers swooped down on Harper's Ferry, seized the government arsenal and threw a cordon of riflemen across the B. & O. tracks. The eastbound night express came to its scheduled stop shortly afterward. The conductor, A. J. Phelps, and the engineer, William McKay, found their train surrounded by a group of angry, shouting men, armed with rifles. Suddenly, in the dark of the night, a shot rang out. The station porter, Hayward Sheppard, fell, mortally wounded. The firing increased, and wild shots whined and ricocheted through the night air. Station Master Fontaine Beckham was hit and died in his tracks. Other train crewmen were wounded as they rallied to the aid of the fellow railroaders. In the midst of the heaviest fighting, Conductor Phelps ordered the train backed away from the scene of the skirmish. Then he sought out John Brown and, after heated argument, secured his permission for the train to proceed. But the tracks were still blocked by Brown's followers, and not until daylight did the night express continue on its way to Baltimore.

When Phelps gave the B. & O.'s president, John Garrett, the full details, Garrett at once notified the Secretary of War, John B. Floyd. A detachment of ninety Marines was dispatched to quell the uprising. Brown and his followers were captured after a hand-to-hand battle, and the uprising was put down. Brown was tried, and hanged within two months, on December 2, 1859. The man who led the detachment of Marines was a colonel who was later to lead all the Southern armies. He was Robert E. Lee.

Within a week after the shelling of Fort Sumter, Northern troops were pouring into Washington through Baltimore. Southern sympathizers tore up the tracks along Pratt Street, and so halted the passage of railroad cars carrying the troops. At that time no steam engines were permitted to operate on the streets of downtown Baltimore. Passengers from the north were transferred across Baltimore by horse-drawn cars.

Greatest destruction to the B. & O. came in the second year of the Civil War. Confederate troops captured the important railroad center

Troops destroying railway tracks.

of Martinsburg. The engine house and engine shop were burned to the ground. The company's hotel, its machine shops, ticket office, warehouse, blacksmith shop, and miles of telegraph lines were completely destroyed. Track was ripped up and heaved upon huge bonfires of crossties. When the rails became white hot, and pliable, they were dragged by chains and twisted around tree trunks so they could not be used again.

Toward the latter part of the war the greatest mass movement of troops by rail up to that time in history took place. Word was received by Secretary of War Edwin Stanton of the defeat of Northern General William S. Rosecrans at Chickamauga in Georgia. He had to have rein-

A train of the United States Military Railroad crosses a troop-guarded bridge on the Orange & Alexandria Railroad sometime during the Civil War.

forcements, and have them quickly, or his entire army would be wiped out. The B. & O.'s Garrett, now President Lincoln's chief advisor on transportation, was called to a conference with General George G. Meade, General Henry W. Halleck, and T. T. Eckert, head of the Army's telegram system. The meeting, with Lincoln in attendance, lasted all night.

The fastest way to relieve Rosecrans was by routing troops through Louisville, Kentucky, then south to Nashville, Tennessee, and into Georgia. The B. & O.'s tracks could take the men to Ohio. There they would cross the Ohio River on pontoon bridges, and entrain for Indianapolis, thence south to Louisville, recross the Ohio and entrain on the L. & N. for the rest of the journey. Eckert at first figured it would take fifty to sixty days for the trip. Since this was too long a period, all participants in the conference refigured the schedule, and got the estimated time down to fifteen days.

Every railroad car in the vicinity of Washington was hastily requisitioned, regardless of type—freight cars, boxcars, coal cars and a few passenger cars. On September 25, the first troops entrained at Washington. Four days later the vanguard of the reinforcements were in Louisville. Within eleven days—four days less than Eckert's most optimistic estimate—20,000 men, 100 carloads of equipment, ten batteries of field guns, plus hundreds of horses and mules, reached the scene of action. This movement is still considered one of the great feats of logistics—the military science of transportation and supply—in history.

At war's end, the B. & O. engaged in its second great troop movement. This was the departure from Washington of the combined Union armies of Grant and Sherman. During July of 1865, 233,000 soldiers left the B. & O. station in the nation's capital. But even after the formal surrender, the B. & O. was frequently plagued by Confederate guerrilla forces.

The Great Locomotive Chase

Of all the railroad tales which grew out of the Civil War, none has captured the imagination as has the tale of the bold and daring theft of a Southern locomotive by Northern spies.

Embankment near Union Mills Station on the Orange & Alexandria Railroad during the Civil War.

The idea itself of stealing anything so large, so cumbersome, so outstandingly noticeable as a steam locomotive is enough to stagger the minds of the most credulous. And to top this, the locomotive was stolen in the very heart of enemy territory, within a few feet of a Confederate Army camp. But the stakes were high. If the locomotive could be captured, Chattanooga, the most important city the South held in the west, could be isolated from the east and the south. Weakly garrisoned, the city would be an easy prey for the Union army of General Mitchel.

Twilight was just spreading over the hills around Shelbyville, Tennessee, on the night of April 7, 1862. Twenty-five men gathered silently at a prearranged spot about a mile east of the town. The man the group reported to carefully inspected all credentials. Then he informed the

group that they had been selected for a highly secret and extremely dangerous mission. Speaking softly, he said:

"There will be no reflection on the courage of any of you who might want to withdraw from this mission. There is every likelihood that all of us may be captured and shot as spies. Any who wish to withdraw, do so now before I explain what the mission is."

War Rides the Rails

The speaker was James J. Andrews, a spy in the service of Union General Buell who had gained the confidence of all Union commanders. A few moments passed as Andrews paced up and down. Not a single man of the 24-man detail withdrew. Andrews carefully outlined his daring plan. The group of twenty-four was to be divided into small detachments of three and four. They were to work their way eastward

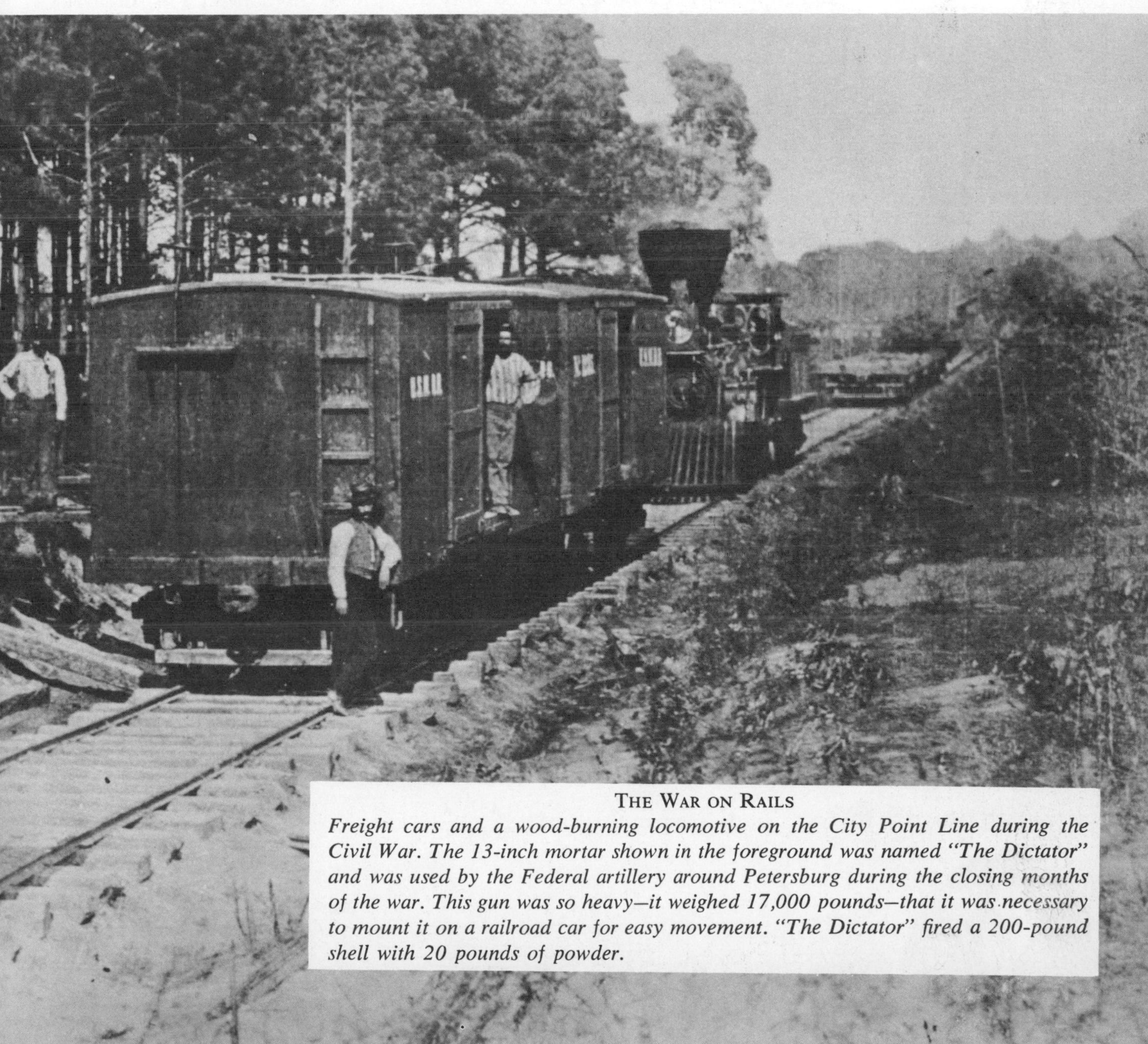

THE WAR ON RAILS

Freight cars and a wood-burning locomotive on the City Point Line during the Civil War. The 13-inch mortar shown in the foreground was named "The Dictator" and was used by the Federal artillery around Petersburg during the closing months of the war. This gun was so heavy—it weighed 17,000 pounds—that it was necessary to mount it on a railroad car for easy movement. "The Dictator" fired a 200-pound shell with 20 pounds of powder.

into the mountains, then turn south, traveling by rail until well within Confederate lines. They were to meet Andrews at Marietta, Georgia, over 200 miles away, on the evening of the third day after the start. If halted, or questioned, they were to say they were Kentuckians going south to join the Confederate army.

Their mission was to capture a train near Marietta, head it north toward Chattanooga, and burn all bridges behind them on the Georgia State railroad and on the East Tennessee railroad, and by so doing completely isolate Chattanooga.

After a few questions, the men returned to the Union camp where they exchanged their uniforms for ordinary southern dress. All weapons save revolvers were left in camp. Quietly, by threes and fours, the men slipped out of camp, on their way to perilous adventure. Two men were captured on the journey and forced into the Confederate army. One man never reached Marietta, and two others who did reach the Georgian town failed to show up for the rendezvous. There were exactly twenty men who met in Andrew's room on the morning before the blow was to be struck, including the leader, Andrews.

Some of the men had made their way to Marietta by taking the train from Chattanooga. They reported that all trains were jam-packed with Confederate soldiers. This would make the mission even more difficult. Then, and not until then, was it learned that the station where the train was to be captured—Big Shanty—had recently been made into a Confederate camp. Some of the men were for giving the plan up. But Andrews announced that he was going to succeed or die in the attempt, and again offered the privilege of withdrawing to any who wished to pull out. None did. With final instructions issued, the meeting broke up. The men hurried to the ticket office and bought tickets for different stations along the line on the way to Chattanooga.

The ride to Big Shanty was only eight miles. As the train rounded the base of Kenesaw Mountain, the Union party could see the tents of the Confederate forces camped at Big Shanty (now Kenesaw Station). Among the twenty Northern soldiers on the mission was one William Pittenger of the 2nd Ohio Volunteers. He described the actual capture of the train, pulled by the steam engine *General,* as follows:

Captain James J. Andrews

"Here (Big Shanty) we were to stop for breakfast and attempt the seizure of the train. The morning was raw and gloomy, and a rain, which fell all day, had already begun. It was a painfully thrilling moment! We were but twenty, with an army about us and a long and difficult road before us crowded with enemies. In an instant we were to throw off the disguise which had been our only protection, and trust our leader's genius and our own efforts for safety and success. . . .

War Rides the Rails

"When we stopped, the conductor, engineer, and many of the passengers hurried to breakfast, leaving the train unguarded. Now was the moment of action! Ascertaining that there was nothing to prevent a rapid start, Andrews, our two engineers, Brown and Knight, and the fireman hurried forward, uncoupling a section of the train consisting of three empty baggage or boxcars, the locomotive and tender. The engineer and fireman sprang into the cab of the engine, while Andrews, with hand on the rail and foot on the step, waited to see that the remainder of the band gained entrance into the rear boxcar. . . . A sentinel with musket in hand, stood not a dozen feet from the engine, watching the whole proceeding, but before he or any of the soldiers and guards around could make up their minds to interfere, all was done, and Andrews, with a nod to his engineer, stepped on board. The valve was pulled wide open, and for a moment, the wheels of the *General* slipped around ineffectively; then, with a bound that jerked the soldiers in the boxcar from their feet, the little train darted away, leaving the camp and the station in the wildest uproar of confusion."

No better beginning for so high an adventure could have been wished for. With the capture of the locomotive, the most difficult step in the entire plan had been achieved. Andrews was exultant as he slapped Engineer Knight on the shoulder and shouted "Open her up!" Knight pulled the throttle lever wide open, and Big Shanty was quickly left behind.

All would have gone as scheduled except for two things: the weather, and the grim determination of the stolen train's conductor, W. A. Fuller.

Conductor Fuller was enjoying his breakfast of ham and grits when to his unbelieving eyes he looked out the window to see the engine of

Conductor William A. Fuller

Andrews' Raiders and the Locomotive Chase

One of the most melodramatic events of the Civil War involved two now-famous Southern locomotives, the "General" and the "Texas." The "General," shown above, of the Western & Atlantic Railroad (now the Nashville, Chattanooga & St. Louis) was captured on April 12, 1862, deep in Confederate territory by a party of twenty-two disguised Union raiders under the command of Captain James J. Andrews, whose intention it was to destroy the bridges along the line. The ensuing chase by the "Texas," shown below, was led by a handful of determined and quick-thinking Southern railroad men who finally caught up with the "General" and recaptured it before the raiders could do any damage. The Union men were imprisoned and seven of them were executed as spies. The locomotives are still in existence and have been exhibited at fairs and expositions.

Course of the locomotive chase is shown in this map.

his train puff by, rapidly picking up speed. With a mixed cry of amazement and anger. Fuller leaped to his feet, tore out of the hotel, and raced to the tracks. There he stood, shaking his head bewilderedly as the *General* disappeared down the tracks. But he didn't stand there long. Fuller was a man of action. Despite the whoops of laughter and hoots of derision sent up by onlookers, Fuller took off after his stolen train on foot. His bandy legs flashing along the cross-ties were impelled as if by springs of steel. Foolish as it may seem for a man on foot to try to overtake a streaking locomotive, had Fuller not acted as he did there would have been a completely different ending to the adventure of the stolen locomotive.

Right behind Fuller came Anthony Murphy, foreman of the Atlanta railway machine shops. He had been aboard Fuller's train, and when he saw the conductor springing down the tracks, he followed, coattails flying in the wind.

There was no telegraph station at Big Shanty, no way to send word ahead to stop the train. No other locomotive was available for the pursuit. It was leg it or nothing. After racing down the tracks until they gasped for breath, the two men came upon a handcar on a siding. They quickly ran it on the main line and were soon pumping up and down, increasing the speed of their pursuit. But the *General* was fast outdistancing the two men chasing it.

Back in the *General*'s swaying cab, Andrews carefully studied the timetable for that day's operation on the line. By closely following the schedule, there would be no danger of a head-on collision with an oncoming train on the single track road. There were two passenger trains to be met at designated sidings, and an unscheduled freight train. The latter, though, not too far from Big Shanty, could also be passed on a siding if the *General* kept strictly to its timetable. Once these three trains had been passed, it would be full throttle, running at the highest speed to the Oostenaula and Chickamauga bridges. These would be burned, thus eliminating all possibility of pursuit by rail and completely cutting off Chattanooga from communication by rail. By the end of the day, Andrews and his daring band would have accomplished their mission.

A picket on duty.

What Stopped Andrews' Plan

All this would have happened except for Conductor Fuller and the weather. It had been raining since early morning. The day before, Friday—when the start of the expedition had been originally scheduled—had been fair. All trains had run on time. The road was in perfect order. But the one-day delay, necessitated by late word Andrews received as to the stage of advance by Union General Mitchel toward Chattanooga, was to throw everything into disorder. Trains were way off schedule. Two "extras" were steaming from Chattanooga toward the onrushing *General*. Andrews, of course, had no way of knowing this.

Every few miles, the *General* would be braked to a stop, and telegraph wires would be ripped down. At one point, not too far distant from Big Shanty, a section of track was torn up. Conductor Fuller and Foreman Murphy, pumping away furiously at the handles of their handcar, hit this torn up section full speed and were sent tumbling head over heels down an embankment. Undaunted, they picked themselves up, ignored their bruises and scratches, righted their handcar, and proceeded with considerable more caution until they reached Etowah Station where they got the first big break for their desperate pursuit.

Andrews and his crew had passed Etowah some time before. An old locomotive, *Yonah,* owned by an iron company, had been standing on a siding, steam up, but Andrews, not wishing to cause undue alarm this early in the game, passed it by unharmed. This was the first mistake. Fuller and Murphy on reaching Etowah, immediately pressed the *Yonah* into service, loaded it with Confederate troops, and now were able to take out after the *General* with a vengeance. Even though the *Yonah* was an old locomotive, Fuller ordered its firebox filled with pitch-pine until its boilers screamed with steam pressure and the old *Yonah* sped down the track faster than it had ever run before.

At Kingston, Georgia, thirty miles from Big Shanty, Andrews and his band ran into the first of the many difficulties which were to plague their mission. Here they met a train from Rome, Georgia, waiting on a siding for the morning mail train—the very train Andrews had captured. From the conductor of the Rome train, Andrews learned that the local freight train was not far behind. There was nothing for An-

The Texas *catching up with the* General.

drews to do but pull onto the siding and wait for it. When it arrived, not long afterward, Andrews saw to his great surprise and disappointment that it was flying a red flag, the signal that another train was not far behind. Furious, his temper near the boiling point, Andrews strode over to the freight train's conductor and demanded: "What does this mean! Having the road blocked in this manner when I have orders to take this powder to General Beauregard without a minute's delay!" This was the story Andrews used throughout the trip: that he was an agent for the Southern General Beauregard bringing an emergency train of powder to that beleagured general.

The conductor's reply was that General Mitchel had captured Huntsville and was moving rapidly on Chattanooga and that city was being evacuated.

The wait for the "extra" seemed an eternity; and when it did puff into sight, Andrews hopes sank even lower. This train, too, was carrying a red flag. The explanation was that, since the evacuation train was too heavy for one engine to pull, it had been broken into two sections, and the second section was not too far behind. Andrews impatience knew no bounds. His fury at the delay increased as his hopes for success waned. Yet, there was nothing he could do but wait.

Not too many miles behind, the *Yonah* pounded the rails with a full head of steam. It was rapidly closing the gap between it and the stolen locomotive.

This delay lasted nearly an hour, but to Andrews and the sixteen men impersonating Beauregard's powder in the boxcar it seemed to stretch on forever. Finally, the whistle of the second "extra" was heard, and it had no sooner gone past the siding than Andrews ordered his train back on the main line, and it was off again. He expected no further difficulties, and the *General* sped away toward the Chickamauga.

What Andrews didn't know—couldn't know—was that Fuller on the *Yonah* reached Kingston only four minutes after the *General* pulled out. Confronted with three trains headed the wrong way, Conductor Fuller acted with immediate dispatch. The Rome train was on the siding, the two freights on the main line. Fuller ordered the engine and one car of the Rome train uncoupled, transferred his troops, and was off in hot pursuit.

Andrews' men trying to obstruct the path of the pursuing Texas.

Four miles out of Kingston, the *General* was again stopped by Andrews' orders. Out piled the men in the boxcar. Telegraph wires were cut. Then the men started taking up a rail in order to insure the stoppage of all pursuit. Just as they were heaving with all their strength, they heard the distant, but distinct sound of the whistle of the pursuing train. Startled, they released their grasp on the rail as it broke and went tumbling helter-skelter backward. Andrews snapped his command to reboard the train, and the *General* sped away, only minutes ahead of its pursuer.

At Adairsville, Andrews came upon a mixed passenger and freight train, and learned from its conductor that an express was behind it, running late. The town of Calhoun was nine miles away, so Andrews decided to take the chance of reaching there before the oncoming express pulled out. The nine miles were covered in less than nine minutes —terrific speed for those days—and the *General* came into Calhoun just as the express was pulling out. A series of sharp toots of the *General*'s whistle halted the express. Again, Andrews told his powder-for-Beauregard story and got away with it again. The express was by-passed. Now the road to Chattanooga was clear of all oncoming traffic. Andrews felt he had won. Nothing could stop him from destroying the bridges at Oostenaula and Chickamauga, he thought. He would soon be able to roll into Chattanooga with the message "mission accomplished."

Andrews was over-optimistic.

Fuller and the Rome train spotted the obstruction of the broken rail in time to grind to a stop and avoid a wreck. However, the broken rail made it impossible for the train to proceed. Once again Fuller and Murphy went into a footrace, but this time they were followed by armed soldiers. They hadn't gone far before they met the train Andrews had by-passed at Adairsville. They lost no time in commandeering it. The train backed up to the siding at Adairsville. The engine, the *Texas,* and its tender were uncoupled. The express passed at this point, so that when Fuller ran the *Texas* onto the main track, nothing remained on the line between there and Chattanooga save the pursued *General* and its pursuer. Streaking along at a terrific clip, the *Texas* rapidly gained on the *General,* since Andrews was still stopping at every station to cut telegraph wires.

Andrews' men taking up tracks.

Beyond Calhoun a few miles, Andrews again stopped his locomotive. He wanted some track destroyed. With this done, he would have a clear way to Chattanooga with all possible pursuit from behind eliminated. The men fell to their job with high spirits. With the track destroyed, their job would be one only of manual labor in destroying the bridges.

These high spirits were short-lived. The men had hardly started on their track destruction when they heard the *Texas* triumphantly screaming as it moved ever closer in pursuit. Another few seconds and they could see the *Texas* bearing down on them at terrific speed. They could see the soldiers on board with rifles leveled in their direction. Another moment and the rail would have been lifted, and all would have been well. But Andrews and his men couldn't wait that extra moment. They scrambled back on the *General* and its wheels spun as it lurched forward.

This scene at a Richmond, Virginia, railroad station in April, 1865, was typical of the destruction suffered by railroads in the South after four years of war.

Union Station at Nashville, Tennessee. This station was headquarters for the U. S. Military Railroads during the Civil War. Note the wood-burner locomotives, soldiers, and tents in the rear.

Since the Oostenaula bridge was but a few minutes away, Andrews ordered one of the boxcars cut loose, hoping it would stop the *Texas*. But the *Texas* merely slowed, picked up the boxcar, and pushed it ahead. Now Andrews was getting frantic. The *Texas* was drawing ever closer. Cross ties, which were to have been used to fire the bridges, were dropped on the track. This did slow the *Texas,* allowing the *General* to increase its lead. There was not time, though, to try to fire the bridge at Oostenaula, so Andrews drove on to the first of the Chickamauga bridges. En route, he had the boxcar stripped of every piece of wood that could be pried off. Then a fire was started in what was left of the boxcar. At a long covered bridge, the boxcar was cut loose. More wood was piled onto the slowly growing fire. Minutes were all that were needed now. The blazing boxcar would set the bridge on fire, destroy it, and Andrews would still have achieved success. But here again, the weather was against him. The wet timbers caught slowly, and even as the men fanned the flames with their coats, the *Texas* came into sight. Andrews had to run for it again.

The *Texas* moved slowly onto the bridge, rammed into the burning boxcar, and pushed it ahead, off the bridge, on and on to the next siding and dumped it.

Andrews in the *General* had been unable for some time to stop for fuel, and now the firebox of his locomotive was nearly empty. Steam pressure dropped until the *General* was slowed to a crawl. Ordering his men to abandon the engine and seek safety, Andrews reversed the *General*. He hoped by so doing it would stop the *Texas* long enough for his men to excape. But the *General* now moved so slowly that the *Texas* picked it up with a gentle bump.

The *General* was recaptured. The chase was at an end. Conductor Fuller, one of the bravest and most stubborn of all Confederate heroes, had won out over the daring Andrews.

The end of the whole adventure came not many weeks later. Since the Northern soldiers were in civilian dress, they were treated as spies. Andrews and twenty of his men were captured. A court-martial was held, and Andrews and seven of his men were executed. Of the fourteen who were never brought to trial, due to the rapid advance into Georgia of Northern forces, eight made a daring break out from their Atlanta prison and reached Northern lines. The other six remained in prison until war's end.

All sharing in this daring raid were awarded the nation's highest decoration for bravery by Congress. The award given them was called the Congressional Medal of Honor, and this was the first time the medal was awarded. This was how the nation's highest honor to the men who fight its battles originated.

Arrival of Lincoln's funeral train at West Philadelphia Station on April 22, 1865, at 6:30 P.M.

331

CHAPTER VI

THE RACE ACROSS THE CONTINENT

GENERAL ROBERT E. LEE, commander-in-chief of the Armies of the Confederacy, surrendered his sword and his armies to General Ulysses S. Grant at Appomattox Court House on April 9, 1865. Shortly thereafter, weary troops of the Union armies turned northward toward their homes; heavy-hearted Confederate troops trudged slowly through burned fields, shelled towns, and devastated plantations to their native Southland, which now lay in ruins.

The great and tragic conflict between the States had come at last to an end. The Union had been preserved. Now it was to be expanded. Now it was to enter upon a period of great and rapid growth.

Not until the Civil War was ended did the long-dreamed-of, long-planned-for linking of the continent of North America by railroad move close to becoming a reality. Although the Union Pacific was formally organized in September, 1862, the first spadeful of dirt wasn't dug until December, 1863, and in the following years, 1864 and 1865, only forty miles of track were laid. The Central Pacific, building from west to east, did little better. Leland Stanford turned the first shovelful of dirt at Sacramento in January 1863. Nine months were to pass before the first track was laid, and only eighteen miles of track had been put down by February of 1864. Not until 1866, a year after hostilities between North and South had been ended, did real progress begin.

Overland stagecoach to California.

The Race Across the Continent

Between Sacramento, the western terminus of the transcontinental railroad, and Omaha, Nebraska, the eastern terminus, were nearly 1,800 miles of the most formidable terrain railroad builders had ever attempted to conquer. The snow-capped peaks of the Sierra Nevadas and the Rocky Mountains reared skyward as challenging barriers. The blazing heat of summer suns were to turn deserts into furnaces, sapping men's energies and spirits. And, always, over the plains and the hills roamed tribes of hostile Indians, determined to prevent the white man from running this trail of iron through their hunting grounds.

The struggle was heroic in its proportions. Mountains were blasted, tunnels drilled, chasms spanned, raging rivers bridged, Indians battled. Slow and steady went the work. As one day of struggle was followed by another of even greater trial, the two roads crept ever nearer their meeting point. And as they progressed, even though tortuously slow, the nation came awake to the mighty battle, and followed it with ever-increasing excitement.

A Currier & Ives engraving, showing the route to California as a train makes its way along the Truckee River in the Sierra Nevada.

Railroad building on the Great Plains.

This dream of an America linked from ocean to ocean by twin bands of steel had been in the hearts and minds of its citizens long before the first survey was run or the first plan drawn up. In the East, the realization that an entire new empire might lay beyond the Rockies did not come until the year 1849. 1849—gold! When word got to the east that gold had been found at Sutter's Mill, the rush was on, and cries soon went up that California must be linked to the eastern section of the nation by rail.

As late as 1862, though, when the United States Government granted a charter for a railroad to run from Omaha to the Pacific Coast, only Iowa and Missouri of the states and territories west of the Mississippi had any significant railroad construction. Four years were to pass from the 1849 gold discoveries until Congress passed an act and appropriated monies for surveys of routes from the Mississippi River to the Pacific. Many schemes were hatched, many bubbles blown up only to burst, many plans advanced only to be discarded, and many years were to pass before actual construction of the Pacific railroad commenced.

By the time Congress granted a charter for construction of the transcontinental line in 1862, the nation was already in the second year of the Civil War. Men who might have helped build the railroad were bearing arms against one another. Materials for the road were needed to replace rails and rolling stock destroyed during the conflict. One direct and immediate result of the Civil War was that the route the Pacific railroad would follow was settled once and for all. For over a decade the bloc of Congressmen from the Southern states had fought every suggestion that the road be built through the North or Middle West. With the secession of the Southern States, this opposition was gone. Pressure immediately built up to have the line run through the northern part of the country so that California and Oregon would remain loyal to the Union.

When Abraham Lincoln signed the law which created the Union Pacific, he was handed an additional problem by Congress—as if, in the middle of a war, he didn't have enough on his hands in trying to hold the nation together. The President was asked to decide what should be the width between the rails

Sutter's Mill

of the transcontinental line. Almost all railroads in the North and East had followed the gauge set by the British—that of 4 feet 8½ inches. Many Southern roads had a wider gauge. Experts predicted that the gauge of the transcontinental railroad would become the standard gauge for the nation.

Abraham Lincoln somehow found time from his duties as war President to investigate thoroughly the establishment of the 4-foot-8½-inch gauge. He discovered that it had been adopted in England because that was the exact width of British wagon roads. These roads had been built to the width of the tracks of chariots brought to England by its Roman conquerors. Chariot wheels had been set exactly 4 feet 8½ inches apart. President Lincoln could see no logical reason for retaining the gauge at this width, and, after long study, he recommended a gauge of five feet. Congress turned him down and stuck with the 4-foot-8½-inch gauge. America's railroads today run on tracks measuring the same distance between them as the distance between the wheels of chariots used by Julius Caesar.

It took many years after the Civil War for all the Southern railroads to change their gauge to conform with the rest of the nation, though. Finally, by 1886, the 4-foot-8½-inch gauge was standard throughout the country, and passengers could ride from one end of the country to another without having to change from one gauge train to another. The Louisville and Nashville Railroad changed the gauge of its entire main line in one day. Starting at sunrise one morning, thousands of workmen fell to, and by nightfall the same day, one rail of the L & N's entire track had been moved 3½ inches closer to the other.

LELAND STANFORD

There were many reasons why there was such snail-like progress on building the Pacific railroad in the years right after the charter had been granted. Shortage of labor and materials was, of course, the main reason during the war years. Raising money to finance construction was still another. Manipulation of the funds raised to build the two railroads was another difficulty. It was only after a good deal of time had passed that it became known how financiers had used railroads primarily to increase their personal fortunes, instead of to promote construction. There was no supervision of these funds in those post-Civil War days, and it took financial scandals to bring about such supervision.

COLLIS P. HUNTINGTON

The Congress of the United States came to the financial rescue of the Union Pacific and Central Pacific railroads. A law was passed granting loans to the railroad of $16,000 per mile for every mile of track laid through the prairie lands, $32,000 per mile for track laid in hilly country, and $48,000 per mile for track laid through mountainous country. In addition, a bonus of ten sections of public land (6,400 acres) was granted for each mile of railroad built. Later, in 1864, Congress raised this land bonus to twenty sections of public land.

The Central Pacific

Four men set up the company which at long last started construction of the Central Pacific. They were to make railroad history, and as a result to become legendary figures in the story of America's growth. Leland Stanford, a wholesale grocer who became governor of California and founded Stanford University, was the company's first president.

Mark Hopkins

Photo taken when the Secrettown trestle in the Sierra Nevada mountains of California was being filled in with dirt by the Central Pacific—shows the meager

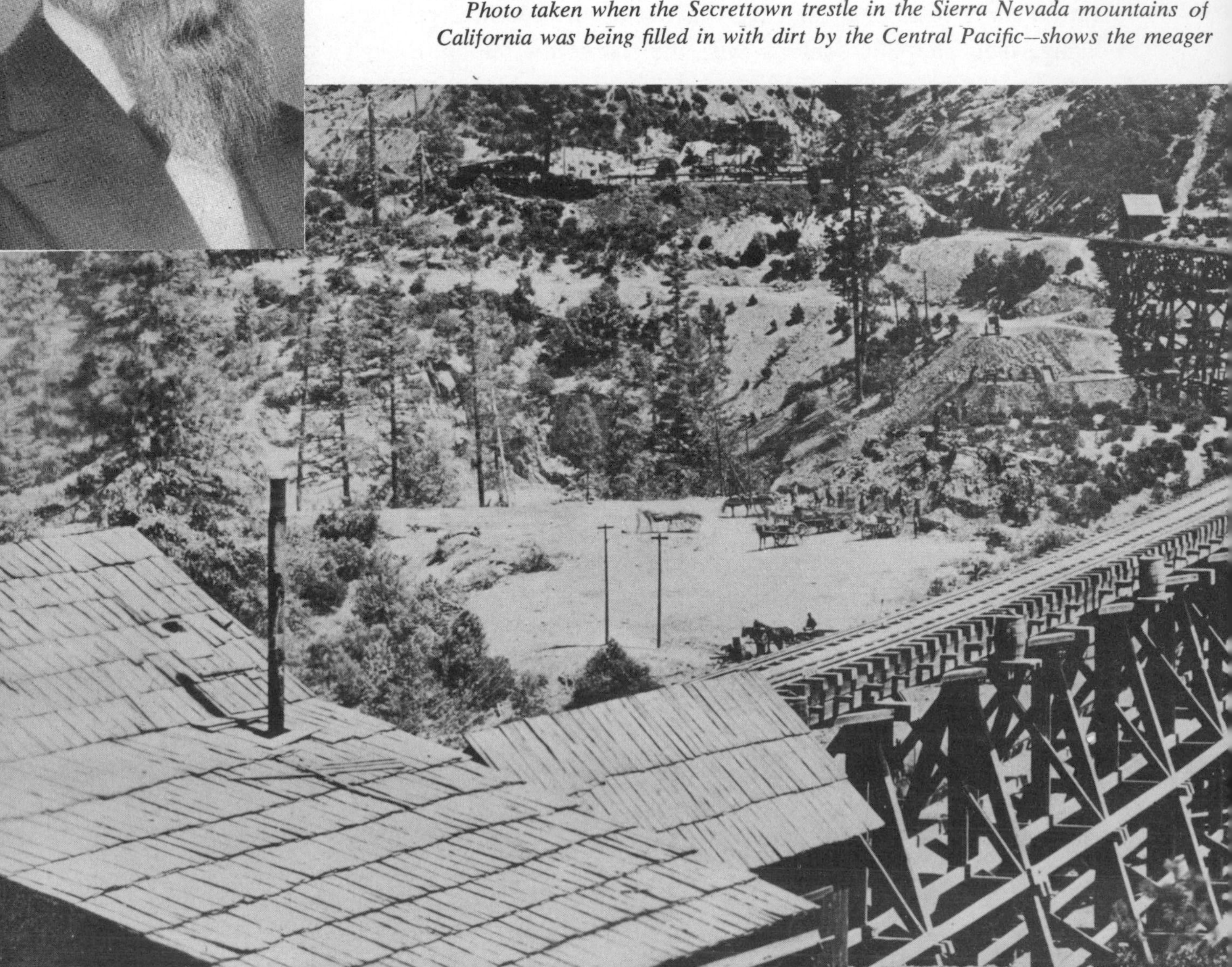

Collis P. Huntington and Mark Hopkins, joint owners of a hardware store, became the Central's vice-president and treasurer respectively. Charles Crocker, a dry-goods store owner, was made a director of the road.

As the day for the start of construction of the Central Pacific approached, Crocker resigned as a director of the road to head up the Central Pacific Construction Company. The stock of this company was divided between the officers of the road.

Two problems confronted Crocker as he tried to get his railroad under construction. One was material. Congress had incorporated into the road's charter the requirement that all rails must be made in America. All rolling stock, rails, tie plates, spikes, and tools had to come by boat around Cape Horn, the tip of South America. The trip took about four months, and the Yankee ships carrying the material had to run a blockade maintained by Confederate cruisers. Some of the lighter mate-

CHARLES F. CROCKER

tools with which the builders had to work in blasting a trail over and through the rugged mountains for the rails of the first transcontinental railroad.

rial was carried across the Isthmus of Panama via a railroad built in 1855, but this, too, was as slow as the oxen, mules, and burros that had heretofore plodded through the tropical jungles.

Labor was another big problem for Charley Crocker—even greater than the time lag it took for his material to reach San Francisco. There were few men who wanted to undertake the back-breaking work of railroad construction when by shoveling gravel in the streams of California they could turn up nuggets of gold. On one occasion, nineteen hundred workmen in one of Crocker's construction camps dropped their tools and took off in a hurry at word of a new gold strike. That left only one hundred men to work on the railroad, and Crocker had paid the transportation of all these men to the construction camp on their promise to stick with him.

It was right after this that Stanford suggested using Chinese labor. James H. Strobridge, construction boss for Crocker, wanted no part of Chinese labor. He wanted strong, beefy Europeans, not the skinny, undernourished rice-eaters, he said bluntly to his boss.

There were tremendous difficulties encountered by the Central Pacific Railroad in constructing the western end of a road to connect with the Union Pacific from the east. In the Sierra Nevada mountains, Chinese laborers fought winter snows that drifted as high as 50 to 100 feet above the roadbed.

But Crocker insisted he try them out.

"Now, look here," he told Strobridge, "those same rice-eaters built the Great Wall of China. I guess they can dig grades for an American railroad."

Within a short time, the supply of Chinese laborers from San Francisco was exhausted. Fifty made up the first labor gang, and their work was so impressive that another two thousand were brought out immediately. Then Crocker began importing Chinese coolies from across the Pacific, until he had some fifteen thousand digging his grades and boring tunnels through the Sierra Nevadas. They earned $30 per month and boarded themselves.

"Give me the material," said Crocker, his labor problems solved, "and I'll build you a mile a day." As we know, he was to do even better, setting a one-day record of over ten miles.

By the end of 1866, the Central Pacific was running trains on a regular schedule from Sacramento to Cisco, 94 miles east. They still had a long way to go, and if their rate of progress didn't improve over that of the past three years, they'd never get their end of the railroad built. But at Cisco, six thousand feet above sea level, Crocker's Chinese construction crews ran up against the granite cliffs of the high Sierras. Fourteen miles of the toughest of mountain terrain lay between Cisco and the summit of the Sierras. Where progress in construction had been slow in the past, it now came down to a crawl. Actually, Summit Tunnel, a quarter of a mile long, took a year to dig. For many weeks, the tunnel was dug at the rate of only one or two *inches* per day. Some help came from a completely new explosive called dynamite, invented that very year by a Swedish chemist named Alfred Nobel. It was also suggested that Crocker and Strobridge use the newly invented steam drill. This suggestion was turned down by Crocker, and he and Strobridge literally hurled their Chinese gangs, armed with picks and chisels, against the rock and granite, working them day and night in shifts. The tunnel was finished in the fall of 1867. Only forty miles of track had been laid that year. But now, it was down the eastern slope of the Sierras, with the desert ahead. The construction pace was to pick up rapidly.

Some workmen on the Union Pacific Railroad.

The laying of the track of the Union Pacific forty miles west of Kearney, Nebrask

The Union Pacific

The Union Pacific had been driving westward from Omaha at a much more rapid clip. True, only forty miles of road had been completed by the end of 1865, but, with the war over, the UP's labor problem came to an end. Ex-soldiers by the thousands, most of them Irish, flocked to the UP's construction camps. The Union Pacific had the same problems of getting materials and raising money as the Central Pacific had. Since

n 1867, is shown in this old print from Richardson's "Beyond the Mississippi."

there was as yet no railroad into Omaha as the UP started laying track, its rolling stock and materials were floated up the Missouri River to Omaha during the few months of the year when the river wasn't frozen over. The rest of the time, the material had to be carted across the barren plains by wagon. So acute did the financial problems of the UP become that there were weeks on end when the workmen refused to lift a tool at the start of a day until they had received their day's pay.

Most harassing of all the obstacles and problems confronting the builders of the UP was the hostile Redskin. Over fifteen thousand Indians, mostly Sioux, fought against every inch of the advance of the Iron Monster. Roadbed diggers carried rifles as well as shovels. Several times a day they would toss down their shovels, grab for the guns, and hold off an Indian raiding party. Hundreds of workmen were killed. Indian casualties were not as high, due to the swiftness of their attack. However, it was figured out by one statistician of the time that in its battle to move west it cost the UP $100,000 for every Redskin who bit the dust.

The Indian had no understanding of the strange trail made of iron which was creeping through his hunting grounds. At first, his only reaction to the weird monster which belched forth flame and smoke as it moved along this trail was fright. Sighting an approaching construction train, Indian parties would wheel their horses and flee into the hills. But, as the railroad kept coming on and on, the Indian lost his fear of the Iron Monster and saw it primarily as a threat to his way of life which was driving the buffalo from its grazing grounds.

Sioux chiefs held a conclave to figure out how to stop the oncoming

Indians attacking workmen constructing the Union Pacific.

of this new enemy of theirs. Their fighting braves sat around them in a pow wow of war. Their squaws had labored long and tirelessly in making a strong thick lariat of woven horsehair. They agreed upon a plan. The time had come to put it into execution. In full war-paint, the Sioux raiding party rode to a small ridge overlooking the UP's right of way. A scout rode farther down the ridge and took a position. Shortly, he raised his hand in signal. He had sighted a puff of white smoke. The enemy was approaching.

The Sioux warriors galloped down to the tracks. Quickly they dismounted and stretched the lariat across the track with thirty strong braves holding on to it on each side. . . . The Union Pacific's work train came plunging on. The warriors braced their feet in the dusty sod. On came the train. About one hundred yards from the Indian's ambush, the engineer spotted the Redskins. He saw the snake-like lariat stretched waist-high across the track. Grinning to himself, the engineer opened up the throttle. In a matter of seconds, his heavy work train hit the taut lariat at forty miles an hour. The train didn't even hesitate as it hit the weight of sixty war-painted Sioux braves. Instead, the Sioux were snapped off their feet, and whipped around until they formed twin pig-tails flecked with Indians stretching out alongside the speeding train. One by one they let go the lariat and went tumbling head over heels amongst the sagebrush. The engineer gave a departing salute to the defeated raiding party with two sharp toots on his whistle.

But the Sioux learned quickly. Soon they were halting trains and derailing them by placing huge boulders or logs across the tracks. They rode their swift pinto ponies alongside speeding locomotives and shot arrows into the engines' cabs. Small outposts of surveyors, and even large construction camps, were attacked with relentless fury. But despite their most valiant efforts, the Union Pacific moved steadily westward toward the Pacific Ocean.

The Cheyennes also made life more than miserable for construction workers on the UP. A worker named Stanley told the tale of William Thompson, one of five men riding a handcar to repair telegraph lines. A Cheyenne raiding party under Chief Spotted Wolf bent a rail on the track, and, when the handcar hit it, the car went off the track. The In-

dians pounced on the white men. Thompson was shot through the arm by an arrow, and knocked down and stunned by an Indian. The Indian jumped from his horse and quickly scalped Thompson. Thompson came to suddenly and saw the Indian ride off. As he watched the departing brave, he saw the scalp slip from the Indian's belt. Once the Indians were out of sight, Thompson went over and picked up his scalp. He carried it to Omaha in a pail of water, hoping it might be reattached to his head. He was to meet with disappointment. The operation by Dr. R. C. Moore failed to restore Thompson's hair. Thompson later moved

Laborers on a handcar of the Union Pacific railroad attacked by Indians,

to England, taking his scalp with him. Years later, he sent the scalp which had been tanned back to Doctor Moore. Today that scalp, preserved in alcohol, is on display in the Omaha Public Library Museum.

As Indian resistance to the white man's railroad lessened, track-laying on the Union Pacific picked up speed. From a mile of track a day, the rate went up to three, four, and as high as six. The Irish workmen were under the command of General John Stevens Casement. General Jack made his men into teams of track-layers, whose precision work rivaled that of the best-trained military squad. Whether fighting

as shown in a sketch from Frank Leslie's Illustrated Newspaper.

Indians, or laying track, they threw themselves into their jobs with a gay mood, and a song that became their rallying cry:

"Drill, my paddies, drill!
Drill, you tarriers, drill!
Oh, it's work all day,
For sugar in your tay,
Workin' on the U. Pay Rai-ailway."

And drill, and work, and fight they did. A writer for the *Fortnightly Review* who visited the scene caught the feeling of the workers, and the vigor with which they attacked their job in these vivid words:

"We . . . stood upon an embankment, only about a thousand miles this side of sunset, and backed westward before the hurrying corps of sturdy operators with a mingled feeling of amusement, curiosity and profound respect. On they came. A light car, drawn by a single horse, gallops up to the front with its load of rails. Two men seize the end of a rail and start forward, the rest of the gang taking hold by twos, until it is clear of the car. They come forward at a run. At the word of command, the rail is dropped in its place, right side up with care, while the same process goes on at the other side of the car. Less than thirty seconds to a rail for each gang, so four rails go down to the minute. Quick work, you say, but the fellows on the Union Pacific are tremendously in earnest. The moment the car is empty it is tipped over on the side of the track to let the next loaded car pass it, and then it is tipped back again; and it is a sight to see it go flying back for another load, propelled by a horse at full gallop at the end of 60 or 80 feet of rope, ridden by a young Jehu, who drives furiously. Close behind come the gangers, spikers and bolters, and a lively time they make of it. It is a grand anvil chorus that these sturdy sledges are playing across the plains; it is triple time, three strokes to the spike. There are ten spikes to a rail, 400 rails to a mile, 1,800 miles to San Francisco—twenty-one million times are those sledges to be slung; twenty-one million times are they to come down with the sharp punctuation before the great work of modern America is complete."

Central Pacific Railroad map of the line from Omaha to San Francisco, published in Harper's Weekly *of December 7, 1867.*

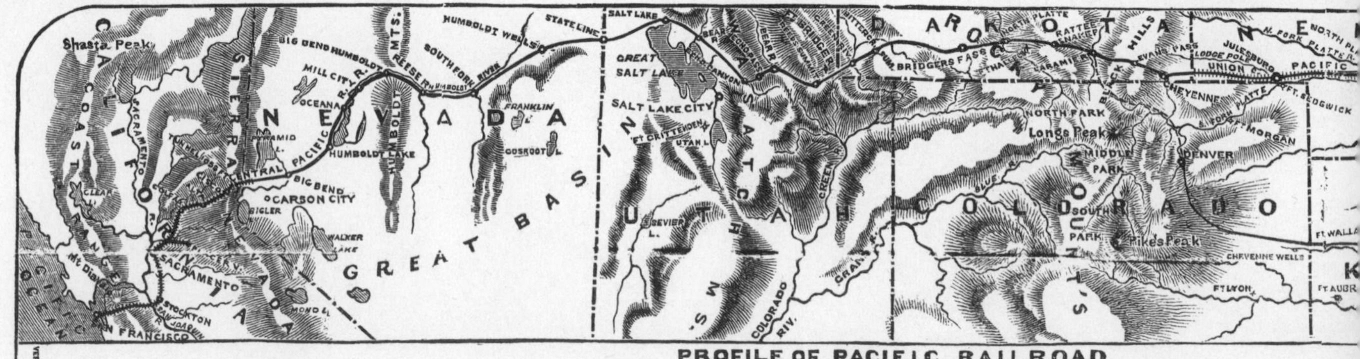

The "great work of modern America" was completed on May 10, 1869, when Leland Stanford drove the golden spike; a golden spike that was soon replaced by a steel one, for even in those days souvenir seekers were on hand. The "Last Spike," made of gold valued at $400, is now on display at the Stanford Museum of Leland Stanford University, Palo Alto, California.

Advertisement issued by the Union Pacific on May 10, 1869, announcing the opening of the first transcontinental railroad.

EAST AND WEST.

Completion of the Great Line Spanning the Continent.

The Closing Work and Ceremonies at Promontory Summit.

The News Flashed by Telegraph Simultaneously Over the Country.

Rejoicings of the Metropolis at the Completion of the Enterprise.

Celebrations in Chicago, Philadelphia and Other Cities.

The Work Accomplished Ceremonies at Promontory Summit.

Special Dispatch to the New-York Times.

PROMONTORY, Utah, Monday, May 10.

The long-looked-for moment has arrived. The construction of the Pacific Railroad is un *fait accompli*. The inhabitants of the Atlantic seaboard and the dwellers on the Pacific slopes are henceforth emphaticially one people. Your correspondent is writing on Promontory Summit amid the deafening shouts of the multitude, with the tick, tick, of the telegraph close to his ear. The proceedings of the day are:

1. Prayer by Rev. Dr. TODD, of Pittsfield, asking the favor of heaven upon the enterprise.

2. Laying of two rails, one opposite the other—one for the Union Pacific Railroad, and one for the Central Pacific Railroad.

3. Presentation of spikes to the two Companies—on the part of California by Dr. HARKNESS, on the part of Nevada by Hon. F. A. FRITLE, and on the part of Arizona by Governor SAFFORD.

4. Response by Governor STANFORD on the part of the Central Pacific Railroad.

5. Response by General G. M. DODGE on the part of the Union Pacific Railroad.

6. Driving of the last spikes by the two Companies; telegraph to be attached to the spike of the Central Pacific Company, and the last blow to announce to the world by telegraph the completion of the Pacific Railroad.

7. Telegram to the President of the United States.

8. Telegram to the Associated Press.

The New York Times dispatch of May 11, 1869, telling the story of the ceremonies at Promontory, Utah.

EAST MEETS WEST

On May 10, 1869, the last rails of the Union Pacific and Central Pacific (now the Southern Pacific) were joined at Promontory, Utah. A train from the East and one from the West halted within a few feet of each other. A memorable scene was then enacted—a spike of pure California gold was driven, signaling the completion of the first chain of railroads to span the American continent.

CHAPTER VII

MEN, MONEY AND RAILROADS

THE WESTWARD race to the Pacific was now on for good. The blows echoing from driving the final spike to give America its first transcontinental railroad touched off the big rail push to the west coast. Men drove themselves in frenzied effort as railroads smashed through mountains, snaked through blazing deserts, bridged lakes and rivers, and overran the impossible in the mad rush to tap the newly-found wealth of California and of the Pacific Northwest.

Within two decades of that historic day at Promontory Point, four additional railroads were operating through lines to the Pacific States. The Santa Fe (Atchison, Topeka and Santa Fe) came out of Kansas, cut across the middle of the great Southwest, and rolled up the center of California to San Francisco. The Southern Pacific went even deeper south into the states of Arizona, New Mexico, and Texas on its route to the great port of New Orleans. The Northern Pacific, chartered in 1864, linked Duluth, Minnesota, with Portland, Oregon, and later Seattle, Washington. The Great Northern shot northward from St. Paul and skirted the Canadian border, cut across the tops of North Dakota and Montana, surmounting the towering Rockies, and reached Seattle.

The advance of these railroads, overcoming every type of physical barrier, fighting financial problems for every mile of right of way, was met by cheering thousands in dozens of cities and hundreds of towns

Iron car-horse and track layers on the Northern Pacific Railroad.

which had sprung up in the 60's and 70's. Those were the years which saw mining camps and water holes grow into the bustling cities of Denver, Kansas City, St. Paul, Cheyenne, Topeka, Portland, Seattle, Duluth, and Minneapolis.

Men, Money and Railroads

It took men to build these railroads. It took money. It took men who could take a dollar bill, stretch it, bend it, use it, reuse it, misuse it, until that dollar grew to be a million dollars. When part of that million had gone not for the rails and roadbeds but into the pockets of greedy men, instead, then more dollars, more millions were found, until the rails and roadbeds finally were down, and rolling stock was rumbling over them. And there were still more millions left over to go into the pockets of those men who saw the railroads not as a means of opening up new frontiers, but as machines to fill their pockets with gold.

It took another kind of man, too, to build those railroads. It took men who had no interest in personal gain, but who thrilled to the challenge of a mountain range, and pondered how to get a railroad over it. It took men who could outlast their Indian guides, and go forward until a lost pass had been found, or a raging river forded. Tens of thousands of such men blasted at stubborn rocks, leveled mountain peaks, lowered lakes, and spanned gorges or roaring waters. They went around mountains; they bored through them; they went over them. They got the railroads built.

CORNELIUS VANDERBILT

THE RAILROAD BUILDERS

These were the days of giants among men, as America burst into the lusty vigor of its young manhood. The years following the close of the Civil War saw the rise to lasting prominence of those who built and financed America's railroads: such men as Commodore Cornelius Vanderbilt, Jay Cooke, E. H. Harriman, James J. Hill, Henry Villard, Jay Gould, Daniel Drew, Jim Fisk, and J. P. Morgan. The battles these men waged among themselves in Wall Street were as fierce as those fought against the elements in the actual building of the railroads.

Cornelius Vanderbilt was one of those who quickly saw that America's future would be tied to its railroads. Against the advice of friends, Vanderbilt sold out his canal and steamboat holdings, although retaining the title of commodore, and sank his already considerable fortune into railroads. Waging a continuous financial battle with Dan Drew,

Jay Gould, and Jim Fisk, the wily commodore built up the Vanderbilt lines through the East, extended them to the Midwest, and formed the New York Central System of today.

Although the Northern Pacific had received its charter in 1864 just two years after charters had been granted the Central and Union Pacific, there was little or no activity on the road until 1869, when the banking firm of Jay Cooke and Company of Philadelphia stepped in. Cooke was considered the greatest banker in America at the close of the Civil War. During the four years of the Civil War, he had sold bond issues totaling three billion dollars to finance the Union's participation in the war.

HENRY VILLARD

Cooke, at war's end, undertook to raise one hundred million dollars to finance America's second transcontinental railroad, the Northern Pacific. His success was outstanding at first, and in three years, over five hundred miles of main line were built toward the Pacific Coast. Then the Franco-Prussian War brought on the financial panic of 1873, and Jay Cooke and Company had to close its doors. All railroad construction came to a halt.

Henry Villard was the man who picked up the financial reins the panic of '73 had forced Jay Cooke to relinquish. A former newspaper man who had covered the Lincoln-Douglas debates, the Civil War, and the Franco-Prussian War, he turned his interests toward railroad financing. By a series of brilliant financial strokes, he eventually became the owner of a little-known railroad called the Oregon Short Line, which gave him a connection with the Union Pacific. But his eyes were on larger things. He wanted control of the Northern Pacific, which was still creeping westward at a snail's pace. The most remarkable thing about Villard was the confidence he inspired in financial circles. Without giving any inkling as to what he intended doing with the money, he wrote to fifty wealthy friends, asking each to subscribe a certain amount of money to a pool of eight million dollars he was forming. He'd tell them later what the money was for. The money came in by return mail. Then, still not telling his friends what he intended doing with the money, he asked his friends for an additional twelve million. This money came in without a single doubting inquiry.

With his "blind pool" of twenty million dollars, Villard bought control of the Northern Pacific. Now Villard began to build. Under his skilled and driving direction, the road from Lake Superior to Portland, Oregon, was completed on September 8, 1883, with General Ulysses S. Grant driving the last spike.

Although financiers played the more spectacular part in the building of America's transcontinental railroads (you can't build a railroad without money), there were among them men who combined the necessary financial skill with a true knowledge and interest in the actual construction and operation of railroads. Among these was E. H. Harriman. He was the man who took over the bankrupt Union Pacific and built it into one of the finest railroads in the country.

EDWARD H. HARRIMAN

Harriman took over on New Year's Day in 1898. He immediately determined to find out just what sort of a railroad he had. He had an observation car hooked ahead of a locomotive, and, with his two daughters for company, he had himself pushed over every inch of the UP's right of way. He inspected rails and roadbeds. He stopped off at every important station, and talked to division superintendents, humble employees, and shippers. Word quickly got around that an entirely new type of railroad financier had arrived on the scene. It wasn't long before engineers and firemen, track walkers and station agents admitted that here was a man who knew more about railroading than they did.

Harriman had grades reduced. He junked most of the UP's rolling equipment, and purchased new, heavy engines, more comfortable passenger cars, and better freight carriers. He had new and heavier rails laid. He abandoned more than one hundred and fifty miles of track between Omaha and Ogden, and built a new line, forty miles shorter. He spent money recklessly, but with a sure touch. He was informed that eighteen millions dollars was available for improvement on the Central Pacific (now under Harriman's control) between Omaha and San Francisco. The general manager of the line asked Harriman over what period of time he wanted the money spread.

"Spend it all in a week—if you can," was Harriman's reply.

Before his career was ended, Harriman had gained control of several eastern railroads, and thus became the first man to direct the destinies of railroads stretching from the Atlantic to the Pacific Ocean.

The entire nation followed Harriman's career. *McClure's Magazine* in 1909 gave a true picture of the man and his accomplishments when it stated: "In comparison with him, the Vanderbilts, the Goulds, the Garretts, the Huntingtons represent the parochial period in our railroad history. They consolidated small railroads into kingdoms; Harriman is federating their kingdoms into empires."

JAMES J. HILL

James J. Hill and the Great Northern

Alongside Harriman, considered the most powerful railroad tycoon the world has ever known, stood another man, a pioneer railroad builder who butted heads with Harriman. The decision was considered a draw. This man was James J. Hill. For all Harriman's fame, power, and skill, still Hill is remembered by most as the outstanding railroad builder in American history. Where Harriman took over railroads already in operation, rebuilt and improved them, Hill, with an almost equal financial skill, and a greater knowledge of railroad construction, built original railroads. He built them against all odds, physical and financial.

James J. Hill not only built railroads, he helped change the face of America. He exerted a strong influence in developing the lands through which his railroads ran. He brought in emigrants by the thousands, and helped them develop barren wastelands into fields of golden wheat, acres of apple orchards, and mine fields which gave the nation coal and ore. Hill was considered to have exerted such great influence in building up the great Northwest that he has often been called the man who made the Northwest.

Hill's greatest triumph was the building of the Great Northern Railroad.

James J. Hill, born in Canada in 1838, came to St. Paul when he was eighteen years old to join up with an expedition of trappers heading for the Red River. He arrived a few days after the last expedition of the year had departed. Hill decided to stay in St. Paul, and within a short time he was an expert in river shipping on the Mississippi. St. Paul had formerly been named "Pig's-eye," after a one-eyed saloon-keeper, and now the re-named, bustling town of St. Paul was to feel the influence of another one-eyed man—Hill. Hill had lost one eye in a game of bow and arrows when a child.

Within a few years of his arrival in St. Paul, Hill was on his way. He had quickly built up a reputation as an energetic and skillful businessman, and had already amassed the fortune of one hundred thousand dollars which had been his goal. But Hill was not the type of man who could stop working, expanding, building. He already had his one good eye on larger things.

With three associates, Hill acquired control of a run-down railroad called the St. Paul and Pacific. Although burdened with all the legal and financial matters of the railroad, Hill soon showed that he was a railroad builder as well. He was pushing his road up the Red River for a connection with the Canadian Pacific, which was then building to the west.

Hill directed most of the building of his railroad in person. He was up ahead with the surveyors, then back with the graders and track layers. He seemed to be everywhere at once. Hill had a minimum goal of a mile of track a day, and this he met, even if it meant driving his work crews to exhaustion. When a work crew would quit, Hill would have another recruited in Minneapolis or St. Paul, prepay their fares, and station an armed guard at the doors of the railroad cars to prevent the men from leaving before they reached the work site.

Daniel Drew

Although Hill drove his men, they respected him, and performed superhuman feats of labor for him. He knew most of them, from ax-wielders to pick-handlers, by their first names. Once, when snow had slowed work to a stop, Hill climbed down from his private car, and spent hours shoveling snow himself, spelling first one man, then another. The men relieved were sent back to Hill's private car for coffee and rest, as their boss took over their jobs.

Hill drove his men through the hot summer months when swarms of mosquitoes on the blistering prairie drove men and animals almost wild. Rattlesnakes were a constant menace. But Hill got his railroad built, and by January of 1879, Hill's trains were making a through run from St. Paul to Winnipeg, Canada.

This was but the beginning for Railroader James J. Hill. He had long set his sights toward Puget Sound, and even as he was building toward the Canadian border, and making millionaires of his associates as well as himself, Hill's dream, ever foremost in his mind, was of a railroad cutting across the top of the states and territories bordering Canada into the Pacific Northwest.

When Hill finally announced his long secret desire to build a railroad across the top of the United States to the Pacific Coast, his friends, as well as his enemies, shook their heads. It was folly, they said. The wild reaches of Dakota, Montana, and Idaho had to be crossed before reaching Washington, and once there, some four hundred miles of rugged mountain territory would still have to be conquered before reaching Puget Sound. And towering skyward, more menacing than anything else, was the Continental Divide of the Rockies. How could a railroad ever surmount those rugged peaks? And, if Hill did succeed, and few believed he would, could his railroad survive against the already established Northern Pacific?

Hill pushed on. To conquer the Rockies, Hill sent for an engineer named John F. Stevens. Stevens' job was to find a "lost pass," which supposedly followed the Marias River. Hill wanted to run his railroad directly west from Harve, in Montana, across the Rockies through the shortest and lowest pass in the Continental Divide. Stevens set out to find the "lost pass" which would make Hill's wish possible.

Stevens started with a plug of tobacco, some hardtack, and one man in a wagon pulled by a mule. He scoured the Rockies to find this pass. His man soon gave up in the face of endless blizzards, and Stevens tried to hire a Blackfoot Indian as a guide. The Blackfoot tribe wanted

Railroad tycoon James J. Hill (sixth from left) and his associates pose in front of the Wm. Crooks, Number One locomotive of the Great Northern Railway.

no part of such a hazardous undertaking, and Stevens finally was able to get a Flathead Indian to go along with him. In the winds of a winter of daily, driving snow, high in the Rockies, the Flathead told Stevens he could go no further. On snowshoes he made himself, Stevens went on alone, leaving the Indian in a makeshift camp. Days later, with no sleep, for Stevens had to keep awake at night or freeze to death, he walked right into Marias, the "lost" pass. Stevens pushed on west for several days more until he was convinced he had crossed the Divide. Then he returned, found his half-frozen Indian guide, and the two returned to the civilization of the Indian Agency.

The Great Northern track layers and graders took the course laid out by Stevens, and the Rockies were conquered.

Hill's Great Northern Railroad was completed when the last rail on the 834-mile run from Havre, Montana, to Everett on Puget Sound was laid January 5, 1893. By July of the same year, through train service was established between St. Paul and Seattle. Hill's line from St. Paul to Seattle, 1,816 miles, was 115 miles shorter than that of the Northern Pacific.

JAY GOULD

In that same year which marked Hill's triumph, the Santa Fe, the Union Pacific, and the Northern Pacific Railroads went into the hands of receivers. Only Hill's line withstood the ravages of 1893, and it was the one transcontinental railroad which operated at a profit for its builder.

There were many sides to the character of this great railroad builder. He could be generous and he could be vindictive. Once, when residents of a small resort town complained that their sleep was being disturbed by Hill's trains running through at night, Hill had the town's railroad station torn down and moved some three miles away. Summer visitors had to ride the last part of their journey to their retreat in horse-drawn carriages.

JAY COOKE

Hill bested Jay Gould on one occasion, when Gould was trying to block the Great Northern from crossing Montana. Hill made a quick trip to New York, stormed into Gould's office, but was told Gould could not see him. Nothing stopped Hill. He forced his way through the outer offices and bearded Gould in his private den. What the startled Gould saw when he looked up as his office door burst open was described by R. F. Dribble in *Strenuous Americans* as "a veritable gorilla of a man, with an abnormally long torso and abnormally short legs, with a prodigiously heavy chest and neck, with thick, sinewy arms, and limbs like granite columns. The great, dome-like head shook so vigorously that the long, tangled iron-grey hair and the bristling iron-grey beard tossed violently about; and the one good eye blazed like a living coal, until it seemed to bore and burn its way straight to the center of Gould's wizened soul. Then the beard burst asunder, the thick lips snarled back, and from between the huge teeth there came a succession of hoarse, growling barks."

J. P. MORGAN

Those "barks" along with Hill's driving force defeated Gould.

Hill, in partnership with J. P. Morgan, gained control of the Northern Pacific and the Burlington Railroads, following a fight with Harriman which ended in a standoff. Hill ran these three lines in his own dynamic way, and his ways paid off.

Hill died on May 29, 1916, at the age of seventy-eight. Ten days before, he had put in a full day at his office. No finer epitaph to Hill's greatness has been written than the words in his obituary appearing in *The New York Times:* "Greatness became him, and was a condition of his errand here. Whatever he had done, it had been greatly done."

CHAPTER VIII

A MAGIC CARPET OF IRON

THE GREAT continent of North America was now crisscrossed with railroads. From New England to Florida, from the Great Lakes to the Gulf of Mexico, from the Atlantic to the Pacific oceans, iron rails were carrying Americans in ever-increasing numbers. Travel has always been a favorite hobby of the American citizen, from the days of the horse-drawn stagecoach through the growth of the railroad, the automobile, the bus, and the airplane.

It was the railroad, though, which made possible the big boost in travel. Where once it took days to travel the two hundred miles between Boston and New York, now the adventure-hunting traveler could cover a thousand miles in a fraction of that time. And traveling by rail *was* an adventure. In the 70's, 80's, and 90's, as the iron rails snaked themselves into wild and remote spots, taking a trip by train held all the appeal of today's Carribean or Mediterranean cruise by luxury liner.

True, the primary function of this new magic carpet of iron was to haul foodstuffs, coal, and other essential freight, as well as the businessmen concerned with the making and selling of these products. Of nearly equal importance was the railroad's traffic in the thrill-seeking adventurer, the man who wanted to "take a train trip," for himself and family.

Whether businessman, drummer, or tourist, the traveler in the early days of transcontinental railroads had to be a pretty rugged individual. The cars in which he rode and the rails over which he was carried were still years away from the smooth-riding roadbeds and deep-cushioned coaches and parlor cars of today. Usually the coaches were either un-

bearably hot and stuffy, or miserably cold and damp. The obtaining of food en route was always a problem, and sleeping, before the Pullman car, was nerve-wracking, torturing, and of constant interruption.

Yet in the thirty years between the driving of the golden spike at Promontory and the opening of the twentieth century, nearly all advances and improvements in rolling stock and roadbeds were made. The major exceptions, of course, were air-conditioning and streamlined trains.

The emphasis in the early days was on speed. Today our trains run but little faster than they did in the 80's and the 90's. Many don't run as fast. In 1884 there was a train on the Old Colony line, called the *Dude*, which made the 72-mile run from Boston to Wood's Hole on Cape Cod in one and a half hours. The *Cranberry Special* which makes

The "Pioneer," first sleeping car built from the ground up by George M. Pullman, was placed in service in the spring of 1865. Its first trip was in the special train which carried the body of President Lincoln from Chicago to Springfield, Illinois. Costing $20,000, the "Pioneer" was the last word in sleeping-car comfort when it was built. According to Joseph Husband in "The Story of the Pullman Car," so well were its dimensions calculated by Pullman that the "Pioneer" immediately became the model by which all railroad cars were measured.

the same run today doesn't do it as fast. Eight years earlier, in 1876, a special train made the run of 3,313 miles between New York and San Francisco in three days, twelve hours, and seventeen minutes. The same trip today, on the fastest, extra-fare trains, can be made in just about eighteen hours less time. Comfort, though, on such a trip has been improved greatly.

Some of the outstanding advances made during those years were: the introduction of the Pullman sleeping car; the sorting of U. S. mail

on fast-moving trains; the invention and use of the Westinghouse air brake; and the utilitarian cattle train. The gaudy, glamorous circus train came into being in 1872. In 1875, locomotives of the Pennsylvania railroad started scooping up water from tanks laid between the rails while traveling at full speed. Steam heat, supplied by the locomotive, replaced unpredictable, flammable stoves.

The Pullman Car

Although the railroads themselves were much more interested in such operating advances as air brakes, automatic couplers, and electric block-signal systems than they were in passenger comfort, it was the Pullman sleeping car which captured the traveling public's fancy. And well it might have.

George M. Pullman

There had been cars termed "sleeping" cars before Pullman, as early, as a matter of fact, as 1836. For the person using one of these early sleepers, however, nightmares more often than not replaced sweet dreams.

A passenger on one of these early "sleepers" described his first trip in one of them as follows: "I clambered to my perch. The tray was narrow and high. It was like lying with one's back on the narrow plank thrown across a torrent. If I turned my back to the carriage wall, the motion bumped me off my bed altogether; if I turned my face to the wall, I felt a horrible sensation of being likely to roll down backwards to be three minutes afterward picked up in detached portions.

"I lay on my back and so settled the question; but the motion! The American Railways are cheaply made and hastily constructed. They have often, even on great roads, but one line of rails, and that one line of rails is anything but even. . . . When I peered through the zinc ventilator into outer darkness, a flying scud of sparks from the engine funnel did not serve to divest my mind of all chances of being burned. Then there were blazes of pine-torches as we neared a station, fresh bell clamor and jumbling sounds of baggage, slamming doors and itinerant conductors . . ."

The luxury and comfort of the modern Pullman car dates back to a night in 1858 when a young cabinetmaker of New York took a "sleeper" between Buffalo and Westfield on the Erie. He found out that his berth was nothing more than a shelf, and that trying to get comfortable on it was impossible. George M. Pullman quickly abandoned his shelf for the smoking car and sat up the rest of the night. As he sat through the night, he pondered the problem, and his cabinet-making and carpenter skills led him to devise a plan for the first true sleeping-car. He experimented with two day coaches of the Chicago & Alton Railroad for over a year. Installation of his innovations cost two thousand dollars per car. On September 1, 1859, the first two Pullman cars were hooked on the rear of a train on a run between Bloomington and Chicago. Brakemen made up the berths. The first Pullman car conductor was J. L. Barnes, dressed in civilian clothes, but wearing a large and most impressive badge. Barnes, apparently realizing history was in the making, wrote a description of that first run by a Pullman car:

"All passengers were from Bloomington and there were no women on the car that night. The people of Bloomington, little recognizing that history was being made in their midst, did not come down to the station to see the Pullman car's first trip. There was no crowd, and the car, lighted by candles, moved away in solitary grandeur, if such it might be called. . . . I remember I had to compel the passengers to take their

Interior of the first sleeping car operated on the New York Central in the 1860's.

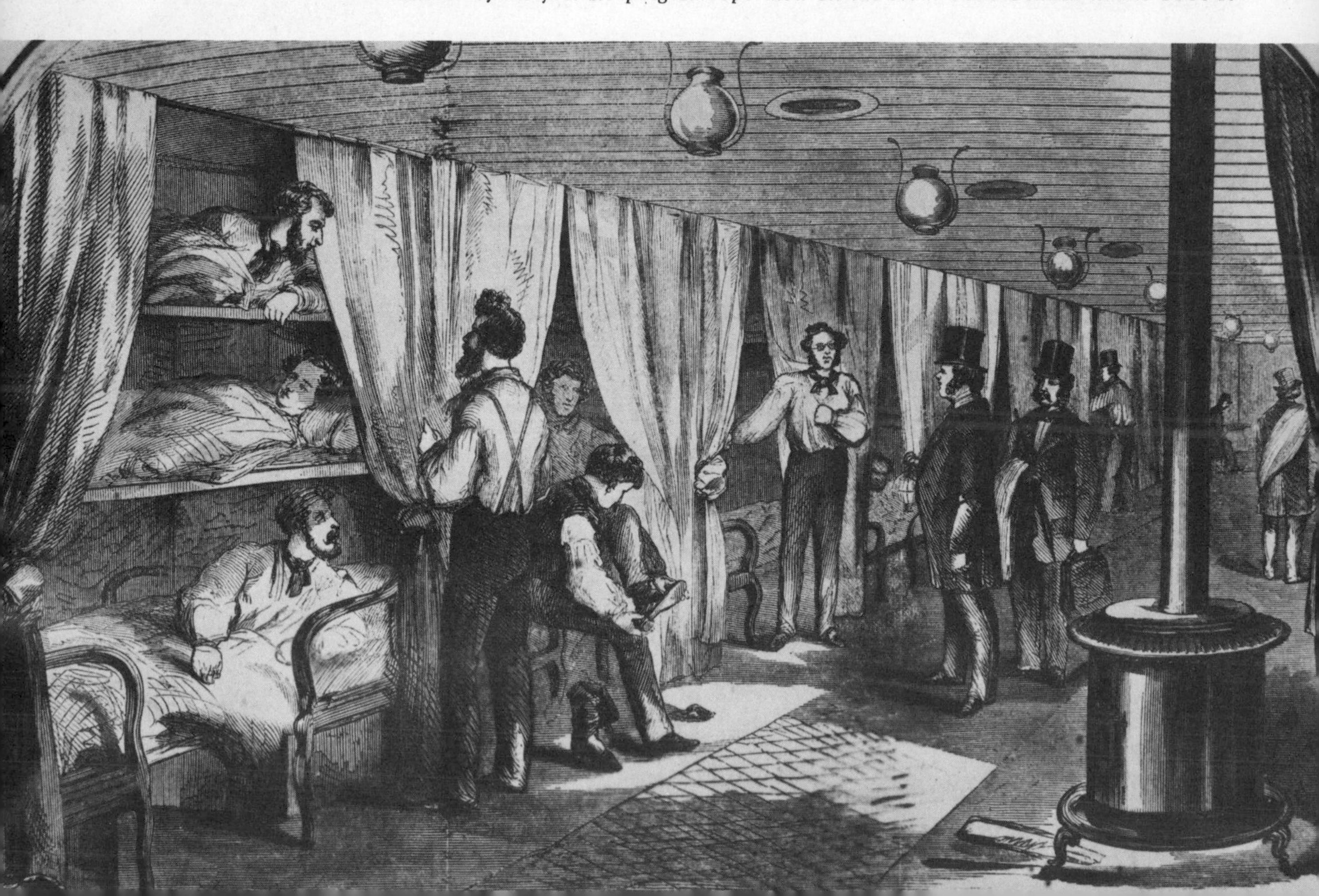

boots off before they got into the berths. They wanted to keep them on . . . seemed to be afraid to take them off. There were four upper and four lower berths. The backs of the seats were hinged, and to make up a lower berth, the brakeman merely dropped the back of the seat until it was level with the seat itself. Upon this he placed a mattress and blanket. There were no sheets. The upper berth was suspended from the ceiling of the car by ropes and pulleys attached to each of the four corners of the berth. The upper berths were constructed with iron rods running from the floor of the car to the roof, and during the day the

Luxury dining on the railroad.

berth was pulled up until it hugged the ceiling. . . . At night it was suspended about half-way between the ceiling of the car and the floor. We used curtains in front and between all berths. In the daytime one of the sections was used to store all the mattresses in. The car had a very low deck and was quite short. There was a very small toilet room in each end, only large enough for one person at a time. The wash basin was made of tin. The water for the wash basin came from the drinking-can, which had a faucet so that people could get a drink."

The first Pullman cars were not a success. Barnes soon lost his job, since there wasn't sufficient patronage to pay his salary. Not until several years later, in 1865, did Pullman build another sleeper which was soon to become popular and successful. He spent twenty thousand dollars on this design, and called it the *Pioneer*. It was called "Pullman's Folly" at first, but within a few months of its first run on the Michigan Central, passengers were fighting for the privilege of paying their two dollars to ride in the car.

Dining Cars and the Harvey Girls

Soon the Pullman Car Company was incorporated as the Pullman Palace Car Company, and as it expanded it started making what it called Hotel Cars. These cars combined sleeping with dining facilities. At first, Pullmans were equipped with a small kitchen at one end of the car, and tables were set up in each section for meal service. From these beginnings there came the dining car of today.

The meals served in those days were not only far more elaborate than the ones served today, but were much less expensive. Passengers had a selection of about every type of game and meat—from buffalo steaks to plover eggs. Here's what the hungry traveler had to choose from in a menu typical of the day:

Prairie Chicken	*$1.00*
Woodcock	*$1.00*
Pheasant	*$1.00*
Snipe, Quail, Golden Plover, Blue Winged Teal, each	*$1.00*
Venison	*.60*
Chicken, Whole	*.75*
Chicken, Half	*.50*
Sirloin Steak	*.50*
Lobster and Broiled Ham or Bacon	*.40*

The Harvey Girls brought a touch of refinement to the "wild and woolly" West. And they also brought the light of romance into the eyes of many a lonely cowboy.

Within a very few years, the hotel car was replaced by the dining car, and for years afterward the traveler with an appetite was offered every type of wild game, as various railroads vied with one another in the elegance of their menus.

Before the dining car took over completely in satisfying the hungers of railroad passengers, travelers to the Far West on the Santa Fe Railroad were fed, and well fed, both as to stomach and spirit by a group of lovely girls who became famous as the Harvey Girls. These were the young ladies recruited by the restauranteur Fred Harvey, whose Harvey Houses were strung along the main line of the Santa Fe. The girls, according to the advertisements offering them jobs, had to be "young women of good character, attractive and intelligent, 18 to 30." The emphasis was on good character. The girls slept in dormitories, had to be in bed by ten o'clock, and were under the ever-watchful care of a strict matron. The girls also had to promise not to marry for one year after signing on for their jobs. This was a very necessary precaution, for men far outnumbered women in the West of those days.

The Harvey Girls were dressed in the drabbest of uniforms, perhaps to detract from the attractiveness which was one of the qualifications for the job. They wore black shoes and stockings, a black uniform dress with an "Elsie" collar, and a black bow. Their plainly done hair was relieved only by a neat, white hair ribbon. Many of these waitresses married wealthy Westerners, usually before their first year was up. Others married employees of the Santa Fe Railroad. Some estimates state that over five thousand such girls found their husbands while serving food in Harvey lunchrooms and restaurants.

The witty American writer, Elbert Hubbard, started the western legend that over four thousand babies, resulting from these western marriages, were named either Fred or Harvey after the founder of the restaurants.

One poet of the day, a J. C. Davis, penned these words of praise to them in 1895:

"Harvey Houses, don't you savvy; clean across the old Mojave,
On the Santa Fe they've strung 'em like a string of Indian beads.
We all couldn't eat without 'em but the slickest thing about 'em
Is the Harvey skirts that hustle up the feeds."

First Through Passenger Train to Sacramento.

SHERMAN, Wyoming Territory, at the Summit of Black Hills, 8,258 Feet Above the Sea Level, Monday, June 7—7 P. M.

The Pullman dining-car International, the pioneer of its class over the Pacific Railroad, is passing the summit, accompanied by two Pullman palace sleeping-cars, forming a part of a through train to Sacramento. Among the passengers from the East are Mr. WAIT, the proprietor of the Brevoort House, New-York; Mr. SWINTON, of New-York, and Mr. SIMONTON, of the New-York Associated Press, with his wife and son; one hundred and forty-six passengers in all. The dining-car seats forty-eight at table at once; is compact but pleasant; has a kitchen and ice-box and a provision cellar beneath. Dinner is now being served, moving across the wilderness at the rate of thirty miles an hour, over an excellent road, in cars free from dust and thoroughly ventilated, with deliciously soft mountain air, the party partaking of as luxurious a meal as any first-class hotel can afford. The vote is unanimous that no railroad travel in America or Europe equals this in comfort or pleasure for men, women or children.

A New York Times *dispatch of June 8, 1869, describing the first transcontinental train ride.*

Glamorized in song and movies, the Harvey Girls have come to occupy a definite niche in the development of American railroads.

Of all the Pullman cars, dining cars, and private cars running over the rails in the United States, none is more elaborate, more carefully inspected and worked over than the "POTUS Special." "POTUS" is the railroad abbreviation of *President of the United States*. This private car used by the President is officially designated "U. S. Car No. 1." It is armor-plated with bulletproof glass windows. Its accommodations include five private rooms, four containing upper and lower berths, while the fifth, occupied by the President, contains a stationary bed with upper berth, dresser, folding washstand and toilet, and a wardrobe locker. A shower-bath room adjoins. The car also contains a private dining room with a seating capacity of ten. Off the dining room are a kitchen, pantry, and observation lounge.

"The Orient," one of the original Rock Island Railroad diners, which operated between Chicago and Council Bluffs, Iowa, about 1878. The first diners placed in service were known as Palace diners, and they were elegant to the last word, with fancy table trimmings gleaming under the gas lights.

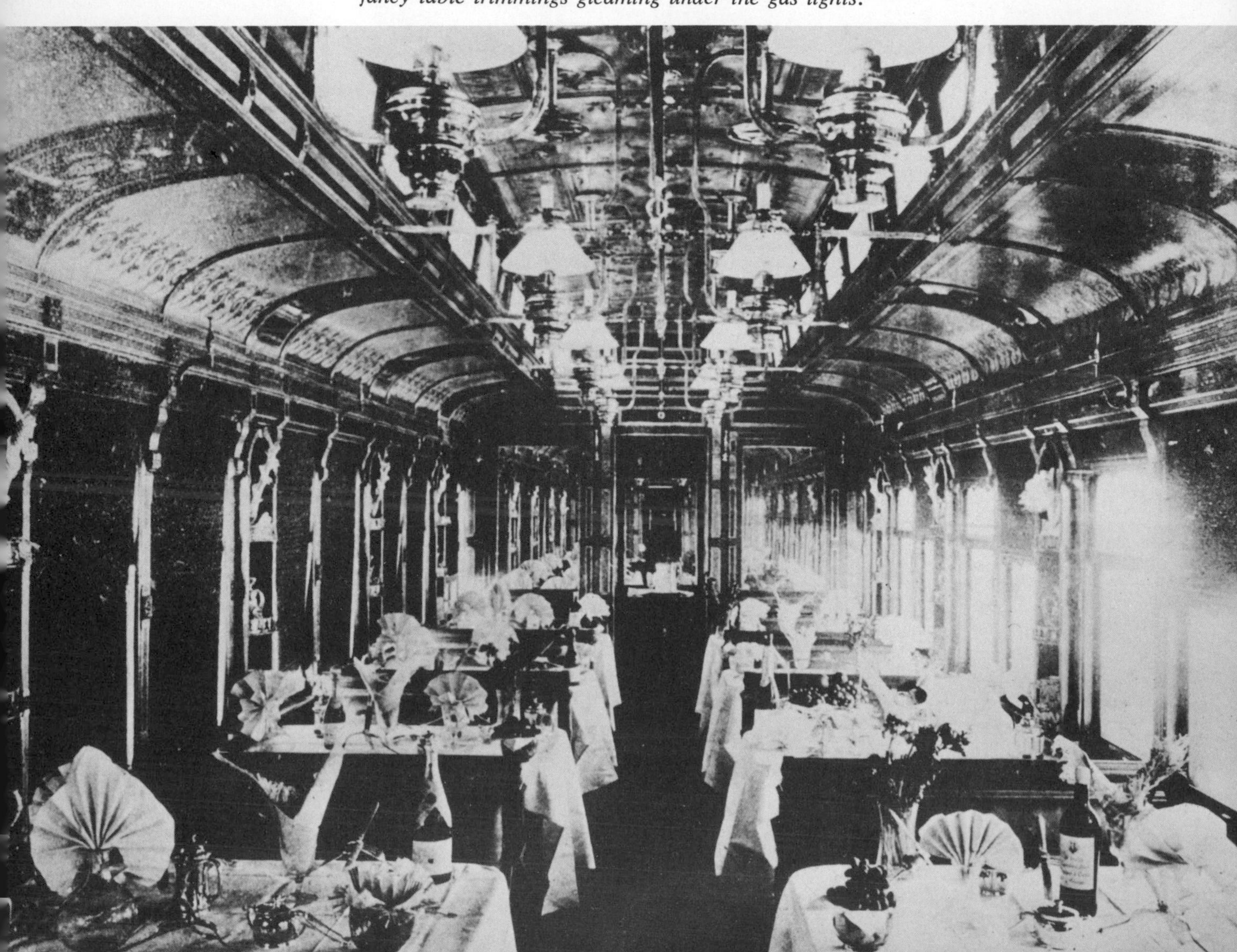

Whenever the car is in use, it is protected by the Secret Service, and the crew is especially selected and assigned to the car permanently. Sometimes this cushy and interesting job has its drawbacks, especially in wartime. The car's staff has to be ready to man the special at a moment's notice, and it is seldom that they have more than this moment of notice.

When President Roosevelt flew to the secret Casablanca conference, he left this country from Florida. The entire train crew was kept under guard behind barbed wire for ten days to keep news of the President's trip from leaking out.

A Magic Carpet of Iron

nterior views of U. S. Car No. 1, he private car of the President of he United States.

CHAPTER IX

NOTORIOUS TRAIN ROBBERIES

There were more than physical discomforts to plague the railroad traveler of the 1870's and 1880's. He could well be riding along on a fine sunny day, trying to get comfortable as he stared out the window at the passing scenery, when, all of a sudden, the train might stop right in the middle of a wasteland. The traveler might wonder why the train was stopping at this desolate spot. His puzzlement could increase to panic as he heard the engine puffing off, leaving its coaches behind. If he stuck his head out the window, imagine his feelings on seeing the engineer and the fireman standing alongside the track watching their stolen locomotive puff away toward the horizon!

Or, again, a train might come to a sudden halt, and before the traveler had time to wonder why, masked men, six-shooters in either hand would burst into the car shouting, "Reach for the ceiling!"

Those were the days of the train robbery, of the railroad bandit and outlaw. Those were the days when a chill of fear would shoot through the traveler at the mention of Jesse James, the Reno brothers, Rube Burrows, the Youngers, and the Daltons.

The first train robbery took place on the Ohio & Mississippi Railroad en route from St. Louis to Cincinnati at the end of the Civil War. The train was derailed just short of its Cincinnati destination. Armed men jumped aboard the train, forced passengers to stand in the aisles with hands raised, then proceeded to strip them of watches, rings, billfolds, and any other article of value. With great gallantry, the bandits refrained from touching the ladies, allowing them to keep their precious jewels. While one gang was robbing the passengers, a second gang cracked open the safe in the express car and made off with a considerable amount of cash.

Notorious Train Robberies

The identity of these, the first train robbers, was never known. It was believed that the gang was made up of army irregulars who had formed into a guerrilla gang at war's end, and then continued their raids in the foothills of Kentucky and Ohio for many months.

The Reno brothers, whose notoriety and ill-fame was just a step behind that of the Daltons and the James gangs, could also qualify as locomotive engineers. One May day in 1868, they made their biggest

Railway robberies became a favorite subject of the Dime Novel during the 1880's.

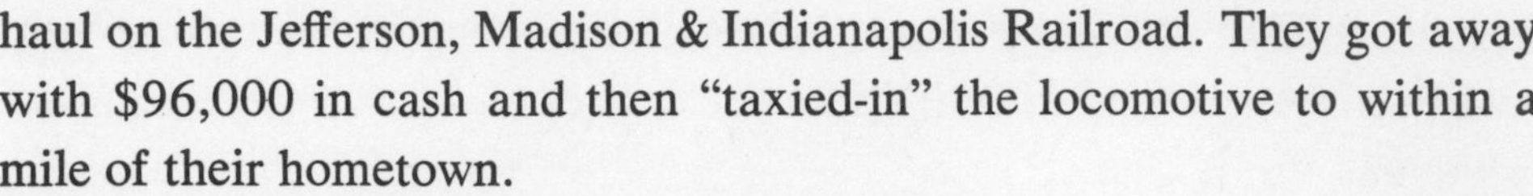

haul on the Jefferson, Madison & Indianapolis Railroad. They got away with $96,000 in cash and then "taxied-in" the locomotive to within a mile of their hometown.

The northbound JM&I was taking on water late at night at a little station just twenty miles south of Seymour, Indiana. As the water was spilling into the locomotive's tender, a large group of armed men boarded the train. One of the group skillfully uncoupled the express car from the cars immediately behind it. With six-shooters blazing away, two other men climbed aboard the locomotive and forced the engineer and fireman out of the cab. Others forced their way into the express car. One of the four Reno boys gave a derisive toot on the whistle, pulled back the lever, and the engine, tender, and express car sped down the rails, leaving the rest of the train behind. The messenger in charge of the express car put up a fight, was beaten until he was unconscious, and then was tossed off the speeding car. He died a few days later. The safes in the car were blown open and the $96,000 pocketed. The Renos took the locomotive, tender, and express car almost into Seymour, abandoned it for their horses, divided the swag and fled into the early dawn.

The Renos were finally captured and hung by vigilantes.

Jesse James was, of course, the most notorious of all the railroad bandits. His last train robbery netted him only $600. During it two men were killed, and as a direct result, Jesse James was to come to the end of his career of terror and brutality.

In the middle of July of 1881, a Rock Island passenger train steamed out of Kansas City headed for Omaha. At Cameron, the first stop, four men walked into the smoker. At the second stop, Winston, one of the men, pressed a white handkerchief against the car window. This was a signal to the rest of the gang waiting at the station. Two men leaped to their feet and climbed on the small platform between the baggage car and the smoker. Two more mounted the baggage car just behind the tender. As Conductor Westphal signaled the engineer to start, he leaped aboard the front end of the smoker. He entered the smoker to be met by the four passengers who had boarded the train at Cameron, each with his gun drawn. Westphal spun around, only to be confronted by the two men—also with drawn guns—who had been crouching on the

The Younger Brothers, the notorious train robbers, were also famous for an audacious bank robbery in Northfield, Minnesota. Top: BOB YOUNGER; *center:* JIM YOUNGER; *bottom:* COLE YOUNGER, *leader of the gang.*

rear platform of the baggage car. From both sides, Westphal heard the command, "Throw up your hands!"

Instead of obeying, Westphal dashed to the rear of the smoker to get help. Bullets caught him just as he reached the platform. He spun, and fell head-long off the moving train into a ditch. A passenger in the day coach behind, one John McCollough, had come forward at the sound of the shots, and was plugged just as he reached the open-air platform. He too plunged off the train to his death.

When word of the holdup reached Harry Thomas, the rear brakeman, he pulled the cord controlling the automatic air brakes and the train stopped with a jerk. Now it was time for the two men hiding on the rear of the tender to go into action. They leaped over the piled up coal and jumped into the cab. With guns leveled at the engineer, they shouted:

"What's the matter? Get going!"

"Can't do it. Someone's put on the automatic brakes."

Jesse James

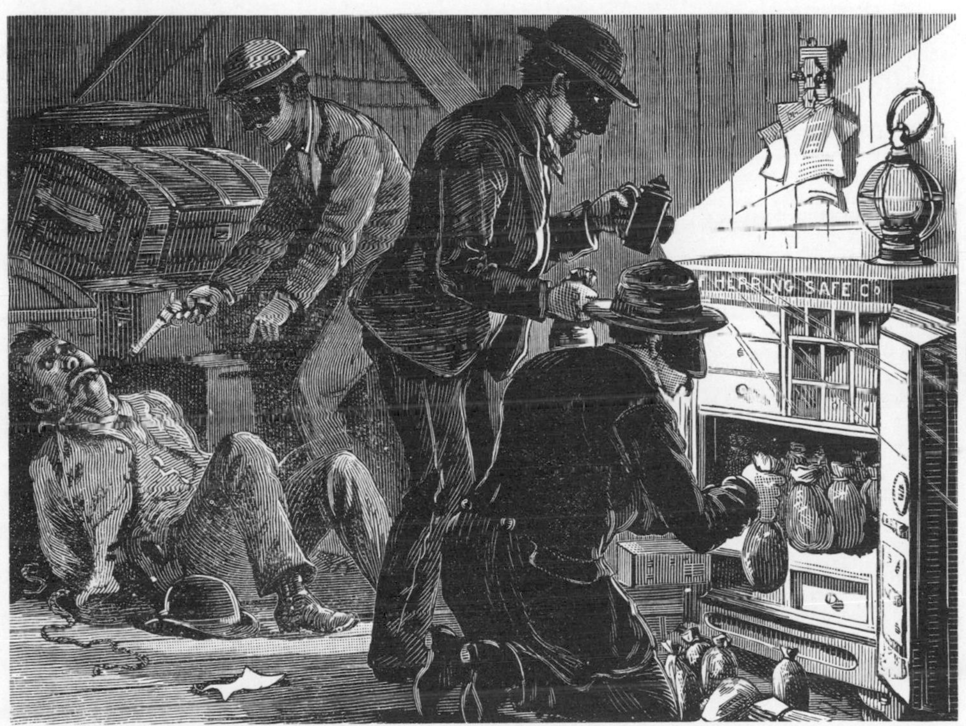

Train robbers at work, shown in an illustration from a weekly magazine of the 1880's.

A shot was the answer to his explanation. It missed, and before the bandits could fire again, the engineer smashed the only light in the cab, climbed out the cab window and clung perilously to the side of the engine. But these bandits were familiar with the operation of a train. Once the air pressure holding the brakes was exhausted, the throttle was pulled open and the train run ahead for several miles. The safe in the express car was opened, yielding only $600. The bandits brought the train to a halt, leaped off, and rode away into the night.

The brutal killing of the conductor and the passenger aroused the entire nation. The president of the Rock Island posted a reward of $5,000 for any information leading to the capture of the bandits. Everyone agreed it had been the James gang. The governor of Missouri offered $5,000 a head for each member of the gang, with a bounty of $5,000 more for Jesse and Frank James. It was this money—$10,000—which brought Jesse James to the end of his life.

In March of the following year, Robert and Charles Ford had become firm friends with Jesse James in planning with him the robbery of the Platte City Bank. Actually, they planned to kill Jesse instead and get the reward. On April 3, Jesse James was in his home. Robert Ford was with him. Jesse now made a fatal mistake. He took off his heavy belt holding his pair of .45's and tossed it on a chair. Then he walked across the room to adjust a picture. Ford pulled out his gun, and, before Jesse James could turn around at the sound of the .45's hammer clicking into the cock position, a slug smashed through the back of his head.

The Fords, arrested for the murder, were pardoned. Frank James surrendered six months later. He was sentenced to life imprisonment, was pardoned many years later, and lived out his life in quiet.

A rhyme of the time about the killing has kept the name of Jesse James alive to this day:

"Robert Ford watched his eye
And he shot him on the sly,
And they laid Jesse James in his grave."

JESSE JAMES SHOT DOWN.

KILLED BY ONE OF HIS CONFEDERATES WHO CLAIMS TO BE A DETECTIVE.

ST. JOSEPH, Mo., April 3.—A great sensation was created in this city this morning by the announcement that Jesse James, the notorious bandit and train-robber, had been shot and killed here. The news spread with great rapidity, but most persons received it with doubts until investigation established the fact beyond question. Then the excitement became more intense, and crowds of people rushed to the quarter of the city where the shooting had occurred, anxious to view the body of the dead outlaw and to learn the particulars. In a small frame shanty in the south-east part of the city, on the hill, not far from the World's Hotel, Jesse James has lived with his wife since some time in November last. Robert and Charles Ford, two of his gang, have made their head-quarters at his house. Charles, it is said, has lived with him in the shanty ever since November; Robert arrived about 10 days ago, and the three have been making preparations for a raiding expedition on which they were to start to-night.

James and the two Fords were in the front room together about 9 o'clock this morning. James took off his belt and laid his pistols on the bed, preparing to wash himself, when Robert Ford sprang up behind him and sent a bullet through his brain. The ball entered the back of his head at the base of the right brain, coming out over the eye. The Ford brothers at once made known what they had done and gave themselves up. They are now under guard at the Court-house. The body of Jesse James was conveyed to an undertaker's, where it was prepared for burial and where a photograph was taken. James's wife has telegraphed to his mother the news of his death. A number of men have identified the body, and there is no question about it being that of Jesse James. A look at the body, while it was being photographed at the undertaker's, showed that he was a fine-looking man, apparently 40 years old, with broad forehead, and his physiognomy was that of an intelligent as well as a resolute and daring man. The house where James lived, and in which he was killed, has the appearance of an armory. A number of guns and pistols, including a repeating rifle, a needle-gun and navy revolvers, with a good store of ammunition, were found there. Jesse was in the habit of wearing two belts, with a brace of very fine revolvers and 25 extra cartridges. In a small stable near the house were discovered several fine horses, the property of James. The Ford brothers claim that they are detectives, and that they have been on James's tracks for a long time. It is believed that they were with James in the Blue Cut train robbery, and that they were influenced in killing him by the hope of getting the big reward which has been offered for James, dead or alive, by the Governor and by the express and railroad companies.

KANSAS CITY, Mo., April 3.—This afternoon, as soon as the news of the killing of Jesse James was received here, Police Commissioner Craig started for St. Joseph with a heavily armed posse of men to guard James's body and give protection to the man who killed him. At the Police station it was ascertained that Bob Ford, a young man who has been hanging about the station for several weeks, was the person who shot and killed Jesse James. Ford left this city about a week ago and joined James in the vicinity of St. Joseph, remaining with him until an opportunity to kill was found. From the Police it is ascertained that Ford, who is believed to be a member of the gang, was under the control of Craig, and has been used as an instrument for James's destruction. Ford is a young man, about 22 years of age, and looks like a verdant youth from the country. In appearance he is a mere boy, and is the last person in the world to be taken as the slayer of the famous outlaw.

The New York Times *of April 4, 1882 carried this story on its front page.*

CHAPTER X

TWENTIETH CENTURY TRAINS

DURING the first two decades of the twentieth century, American railroads reached the pinnacle of their success. They stood unchallenged, not only in this country, but throughout the world, as the finest, fastest form of transportation ever developed by man. The running time of all roads was stepped up in these years, although some individual speed records set as early as 1876 still withstood all challenges.

Train travel became more comfortable—even luxurious—for those who could afford the extra-fare train or the Pullman or parlor car. Coach travel still left a lot to be desired. Seats were rigid, hard, and the cars were often dirty, drafty, and rough riding.

The 30's and 40's saw these conditions changed with the introduction of the streamlined train and air-conditioning, the two major improvements in railroad travel during the twentieth century. Coach travel was brought up to a standard of comfort approaching that of the parlor car. Coaches were built with deep-cushioned, easy-riding, reclining seats; "snack" bars and other pleasant conveniences were added. About the only difference between the coach and the parlor car was that by a reservation one was assured a seat in a parlor car, while coach travel was still "first come first served."

Railroads remain the foremost carriers of freight today, even with the challenge of long-haul, over-the-road heavy trucking. Not so with passenger travel. Railroads began losing their dominant position in passenger travel in the 20's, as buses moved in to take away traffic on short hauls. Although slower, bus travel was considerably cheaper.

The automobile and improved highways also cut into railroad passenger traffic. Papa, mama, and the kids now piled into the family car for the visit to grandpa down on the farm, instead of making box lunches and taking the train.

In the late 30's the airplane entered the travel arena, and loomed as a serious threat to the railroad's travel superiority. This threat, held back by World War II, came to full promise after the war, as air travel zoomed with the speed of its own flight.

Streamlining, air-conditioning, all-coach, fast through trains were the railroads answers to these challenges, but it has been a losing fight. No longer is the railroad the supreme carrier of human cargo. Hundreds of short lines have been abandoned. Many railroads have curtailed the number of runs on their main lines.

The railroads are fighting back, though. Today, with motor traffic increasing by leaps and bounds, particularly in the crowded metropolitan areas, with parking space harder to find than uranium, many a commuter is finding it much more comfortable and much faster to take a Bee Liner or a Budd Liner than it is to buck traffic in his car.

Even today, though, an all-metal, streamlined train speeding across a plain, or winding swiftly through a mountain pass, is a sight to thrill the spectator and start his heart pumping with desire to climb aboard and go somewhere. The day will probably never come when the swift passage of a train—freight or passenger—through a town or city will fail to command the attention of everyone within sight of it. Just as in the early days, when people gathered at the "deepo" to watch the 5:15 highball through, heads turn and attention is riveted at the thrilling sound of an approaching train's whistle or horn.

The announcement by a railroad of a new type of train is still front-page news. That train's trial run brings out the press and the newsreel cameramen. Television flashes on-the-scene pictures into the living rooms of the nation. Americans may not travel by train as much as they formerly did, but their interest in trains is as high today as it was in the days of long ago. There probably isn't a boy in America who still doesn't list a set of electric trains as number one among his most longed-for Christmas presents. Chances are he will get almost as much fun out of operating it as his father does.

Twentieth Century Trains

The decline of passenger travel and the decrease in interest by railroads in stepping up speed can be traced to other factors in addition to the rise of the bus, the automobile, and the airplane. The telegraph and the telephone, particularly the latter, have done much toward eliminating the necessity of a man's going from one place to another to clear up a point regarding a business deal, or for a mother to find out how her daughter's new baby is getting along. Before these two means of communication, the only way, besides the slow mail, to find out what was happening at a distant point was to go there.

That's just what Jay Gould had to do one summer in the 80's when he was at the top of his power as a ruler of railroads. Gould was on an inspection trip of one of the western lines he controlled, when word caught up with him that he had to get back to Denver at once. Stock market "wolves" were beginning a raid on his holdings. Gould was traveling, as usual, behind his favorite engineer, Kid Hadlock, in Gould's

The new "City of Portland" rounds a curve along the Columbia River Gorge. Its dome cars, providing passengers with extra viewing area, are popular with travelers in the West.

Automatic sliding doors at the center distinguish these new two-level commuter cars from other double-decked cars. They carry 145 passengers each, and were custom built to incorporate changes suggested by commuters.

"Chair Car" on Southern Pacific's "Shasta Daylight" which runs between San Francisco and Portland. "Sky-view" windows offer passengers a superb view of the beautiful scenery along the world-famous Shasta route. A special "breather" sash keeps windows free from moisture, providing a crystal clear picture at all times.

private train which carried locomotive, tender, baggage car, and a sumptuous private car. They were one hundred miles away from Denver, in the high mountains. Gould asked Hadlock if they could make it back to the city in two hours. The Kid cocked an eyebrow, briefly considered the down-mountain run he'd have to make, and answered, "If she'll stay on the rails, we'll make it."

"Let's go" was Gould's reply.

To make one hundred miles in two hours, winding through the mountains, even if the trip were *all* down-grade, would be quite a feat. Hadlock was right. Keeping the train on the track was his big problem—or so he thought. What Hadlock couldn't anticipate was an engine truck box running hot as they roared into the final stretch of their down-mountain plunge. Hadlock turned the controls over to the fireman with orders to "keep her rollin'," and climbed out to the front of the speeding locomotive. Clinging on to a guard rail with his legs, Hadlock unpacked the burned out waste in the hot box, repacked it, poured in the oil, and clambered back to the cab as the engine swayed and screeched around the mountain curves.

Gould made it back to the city in time.

Transcontinental Speed Records

Rail baron E. H. Harriman, back in 1906, had occasion to get somewhere in a highballing hurry, too. He was in San Francisco doing relief work in the wake of the earthquake when he was notified that his presence was needed in New York just as fast as it could be delivered there. He ordered his private train readied, and 71 hours and 27 minutes after pulling out of Oakland, Harriman rolled into New York. This was a new speed record for crossing the continent.

Fast as Harriman's trip was, it cut only twelve hours off the record set thirty years before by the Jarrett & Palmer Special, a theatrical train. There were two reasons for this first crack at the transcontinental speed record. One was the desire of Lawrence Barrett, leading man of the Jarrett & Palmer Theatrical Company, to cross the country faster than it had ever been crossed before. The second was the necessity of getting the theatrical troupe to San Francisco for a scheduled opening of Shakespeare's *Henry V*. This show, produced in New York at Booth's Theatre by Jarrett & Palmer, closed in New York the night of May 31, 1876, and was due to open at McCullough's Theatre in San Francisco on June 5.

The average time for crossing the continent in the 70's was seven to eight days. If the curtain was to rise on *Henry V* on schedule, the time for crossing the nation would have to be halved.

Barrett, who often co-starred with Edwin Booth, took his final bows just before midnight, and with the rest of the company and friends ferried across the Hudson to Jersey City, where the Jarrett & Palmer Special was waiting with a full head of steam.

The Special consisted of one baggage car, one combination commissary and smoking car, and one Pullman. Six engines had been carefully groomed and polished to pick up the Special at various divisions on the cross-country dash. Thirty-five passengers were on board, and were paying $500 for the privilege of making the speed run.

The Jarrett & Palmer Special pulled out at 1:00 A.M., June 1, 1876, with Barrett taking bows from the rear platform. He took them at every stop across the country. Exactly 83 hours and 37 minutes later, the Special steamed into San Francisco; this included stops of 2 hours and 3 minutes on the way.

The curtain went up on time.

Harriman lowered that record thirty years later. Twenty-eight more years were to pass before the record was again lowered. In 1934, by running a "special," the Union Pacific brought the record down to 56 hours and 55 minutes for a transcontinental run between Los Angeles and New York.

Barrett wasn't the only man who wanted to hold a speed record. In 1905, Walter Scott, better known as "Death Valley Scotty," also had the yen to "get there faster than anyone else ever had." Scotty was a prospector who had had many ups and downs—mostly downs. He had

The "Empire Builder" near Glacier National Park, Montana

often "ridden the rods" as a hobo over the same railroad he chartered to set a record between Los Angeles and Chicago.

On a hot afternoon in July, Scotty, dressed in a cheap blue serge suit, cowboy boots, a bright red tie and a ten-gallon hat walked into the office of John J. Byrne, general passenger agent of the Santa Fe at Los Angeles, and started peeling off thousand dollar bills.

"Wanna buy some speed," Scotty drawled. "How much to git me to Chicago in 46 hours?"

A low whistle came from Byrne's lips, and he shook his head. "Don't

n its scenic route between Chicago and the Pacific Northwest.

know. Fastest the run's ever been made is 57 hours and 56 minutes. That's a big order you're asking for."

The two men haggled for a time. Byrne called in his assistants. After much consultation, Scotty was told, "We'll get you there if steam and iron will hold together, and it will cost you $5,500."

Scotty tossed the money and asked, "When do we leave?"

By nightfall Byrne had torn the entire Santa Fe system apart. Telegraphic orders went out to every division. All specials, express trains, and fast freights were to go onto sidings to give Scotty's train, called the *Coyote Special,* a clear right of way. Switches were to be spiked a half-hour before the *Coyote* was to roar through.

At noon the next day, Scotty and his pretty young wife fought their way through the crowds of curious sightseers and boarded the Special. Morning newspapers had carried the story of the speed attempt under big, black headlines. One hour later, as the crowds cheered, Engineer Finley pulled back on the throttle of Engine 442, and the race began.

Scotty's special covered the first sixty miles in four minutes under an hour. Plunging through the hot sands of the Mojave desert, Finley pushed 442 up to a speed of one mile in thirty-one seconds. Six hours after leaving Los Angeles, the *Coyote Special* roared through Fenner. There, on a siding, stood the Chicago Express, the deluxe train which had left Los Angeles at 7:30 that morning, five and a half hours before the departure of the *Coyote.*

Scotty was enjoying himself immensely. Part of the trip he rode in his Pullman. At other moments, he crawled over the tender to ride with the engineer, urging him on to even greater speed.

Scotty tossed a telegram from the speeding train at one station. It was for President Teddy Roosevelt: "An American cowboy is coming east on a special train faster than any cowpuncher ever rode before; how much shall I break the transcontinental record?"

At Fort Madison, engines and engineers were changed for the final dash into Chicago. Even with ten minutes lost for engine trouble, and three full stops for water, the *Coyote* made the 239-mile run from Fort Madison to Chicago in 244 minutes. Scotty had made the trip of 2,265 miles in just six minutes under forty-five hours—13 hours and 2 minutes faster than the run had ever been made before.

Chicago gave him a hero's welcome.

Casey Jones

The Story of Casey Jones

Whenever and wherever railroad buffs gather, and the subject of speed comes up, someone is bound to start singing softly, "Come all you rounders if you want to hear," and the name of the most famous engineer in all railroad history holds the scene. His fame is due primarily to the ballad which celebrates his final ride to "that promised land." Casey Jones was this rounder's name and the *Cannonball Express* was the train he rode to fame.

There really was a Casey Jones, and he did go to his death while trying to make up time when behind schedule. Engineer John Luther Jones was called "Casey" after the town of Cayce, Kentucky. Some hold that Cayce was his birthplace. Jealous Missourians say "no," he was born in the southwestern part of their state.

Casey was an engineer on the Illinois Central Railroad. Early in the morning of April 30, 1900, Casey had the *Cannonball Express* plunging through the night at every bit of speed he could get out of her. Casey was at the throttle because a fellow engineer was sick, and Casey had volunteered for the run. He had picked up the *Cannonball* at Memphis, told his fireman Sim Webb to give him steam to make "them

Casey Jones in the cab of engine No. 638. This photograph was taken in 1900 shortly after Casey Jones was assigned to the engine; he is shown seated with hand on the throttle. The man standing in the gangway is J. W. (Bull) McKinnie, who fired for Casey for two years. This locomotive was known for its highly polished bell, glittering hand rails and number plates, and for its wonderful six-chime whistle.

drivers roll," and plunged the long train of Pullmans out of the Memphis yard in a driving rain, heading south to New Orleans.

Driving through the night at more than sixty miles per hour, Casey rounded a curve just north of Vaughan, Mississippi, when he saw a red lantern swinging across the track. A freight, taking a siding to clear the main line for the *Cannonball,* hadn't completely cleared. Two heavy boxcars and the caboose were still on the main track. Casey yanked the Johnson bar to throw the engine into reverse, poured sand on the rails, and snapped on the air brakes. He shouted to Webb to jump. Webb did, but Casey, trying to bring his speeding train to a stop, ploughed into the tail of the freight and took his last ride to that "promised land."

With the coming of the Diesel engine, and the streamlined train, the public has generally come to believe that Diesel-powered trains hold all

The "Pioneer Zephyr" (left), *Burlington's stainless steel streamliner, was the first train of this type to use Diesel power. Scheduled passenger train service began on November 11, 1934, between Lincoln, Nebraska, and Kansas City, Missouri. Here she is shown beside her newest sister, the "Kansas City Zephyr," on the former's 20th anniversary in May, 1954.*

Twentieth Century Trains

the speed records. Nothing could be farther from the truth. Your real train enthusiast who bemoans the passing of the steam locomotive can be heartened by the fact that steam engines still hold the records for the fastest times ever made on a railroad.

The best Diesel speed ever recorded is 120 miles per hour. This speed was matched by steam as early as 1901. A 10-wheeler, coal-burning engine on the Savannah, Florida and Western pulled a mail car, baggage car, and sleeping-car from Fleming, Georgia, to Jacksonville, Florida, a distance of 149 miles, in 130 minutes. One five-mile stretch of the run was made in 2 minutes and 30 seconds, a rate of 120 miles per hour. Four years later, a Pennsylvania Flyer made a three-mile run near Ada, Ohio, in exactly 85 seconds, an average of 127 miles an hour. This record has withstood all challenges by Diesel-driven engines.

Despite the speeds that can be developed by steam engines, Diesel-powered engines had replaced steam on almost all American railroads by the middle of the twentieth century. Efficiency, low cost of operation,

and ease of maintenance are the qualities which make Diesel power preferable to steam. Some railroads have sent all their steam engines to the roundhouse permanently and use Diesel engines exclusively.

All Diesel engines are equipped with what is called "dead-man control." This is a device, either a foot pedal or hand lever, which requires constant pressure on the part of the engineer. In the event of death or accident, resulting in this pressure being removed, every air brake on every unit of the train is automatically applied, bringing the train to a stop.

RUDOLPH DIESEL

Electrification of railroads took great strides in the 20's and 30's. Electric power had first been used in America on street railways. As far back as 1895 it was in use on short sections of some railroads. It was first adopted in that year by the New York, New Haven and Hartford Railroad, and, later in the same year, the Pennsylvania and B. & O. converted part of their trackage to electric power. At first, electrically driven trains were used mostly in urban areas to eliminate smoke and steam, particularly where trains tunneled under cities to reach their termini. The Park Avenue tunnel in New York City which leads to Grand Central Station was completely electrified in 1907, following a serious accident when the tunnel became filled with smoke and scalding steam. In fact, New York State enacted a law prohibiting the use of combustion engines in the city limits of New York City.

It was soon discovered that electric power gave greater traction than any other, and mountain lines began to switch over. In the Montana section of the Chicago, Milwaukee, St. Paul and Pacific, over six hundred miles of mountain trackage has been electrified for heavy freight hauls. The Pennsylvania Railroad operates electrically powered trains almost exclusively on its runs from New York to Philadelphia, Harrisburg, and Washington. Electric trains also have greater acceleration, making faster schedules possible, particularly in heavy commuting areas.

THE STREAMLINERS

The first of the Diesel-powered, all streamlined "wonder trains" was the Burlington Route's *Pioneer Zephyr*. On May 26, 1934, the gleaming *Zephyr* made an historic dawn-to-dusk, non-stop run from Denver to Chicago to re-open the Century of Progress Exposition. It is estimated that over two million persons lined the Burlington's right-of-way for a glimpse of this wonder train as it streaked over the 1,015 miles of track between Denver and Chicago. The average speed of the run was 77.6 miles per hour, and it was twice the distance ever made on any previous non-stop run.

The *Pioneer Zephyr* proved to be an immediate success. In October of the same year, the nation thrilled again to a spectacular transcontinental run made by a streamliner of the Union Pacific. This train made the run of 3,258 miles from Los Angeles to New York City in 56 hours and 55 minutes with an over-all average speed of 57.2 miles per hour.

The success of these trains and the attention they created brought other railroads into the streamlined field with a rush. They couldn't get their orders in fast enough. The Union Pacific in June, 1935, put its *City of Portland* into regular operation between Chicago and Oregon. The Santa Fe soon had a *Super Chief* running between Chicago and Los Angeles at a 60.5-mile per hour average These trains of the Burlington, Union Pacific, and Santa Fe lines were quickly followed by the Boston & Maine's *Flying Yankee*, the Rock Island's *Rocket*, and the Mobile & Northern's *Rebel*. Every road in the nation soon had its special streamliner whizzing over its main line.

Plastic blisters called "domes" appeared atop these streamliners, particularly in the West, as the railroads fought to retain the traffic going over to air travel. Plastic domes give passengers an unparalleled view of the scenery they speed through. Luxury trains became more luxurious. Schedules were cut down to a point just this side of the danger line.

By the early 1950's railroads had reached a point where they were giving the finest and fastest service—more particularly on long hauls—they could develop. But passenger traffic continued to fall off, as more and more people took to the air. The railroads gathered ammunition to continue the battle. Talk shifted from streamlining and dome cars to the "Train of the Future," a train that would provide all the ease and comfort developed thus far, as combined with speeds—even on regular schedules—of 100 miles per hour and better.

THE "SUPER CHIEF"

The "Super Chief," all-Pullman streamliner operating with the most modern train equipment available, runs daily between Chicago and Los Angeles.

304
SANTA FE
SANTA FE

CHAPTER XI

THE TRAIN OF THE FUTURE

WITH the opening of the second half of the twentieth century, American railroads had to face up as never before to the problem of increasing deficits from passenger service coupled with a decrease in the number of persons riding on trains. The automobile accounted for over 90 percent of inter-city travel, and the airplane was taking a big bite of passenger traffic on long hauls. Something had to be done.

Newspapers and magazines carried stories about "Train X," "The Aero-Train," and the "Talgo" train. These were referred to as the "Trains of the Future." Whether such trains will be the answer to the railroads' passenger traffic problem is a question only the future can decide. It will take several years to determine if such trains can woo back passengers in sufficient numbers and operate at a low enough cost to move passenger service out of the deficit column into the break-even or profit column.

The "lightweight train" gives promise of being the answer. This type of train reduces equipment investment, reduces operating and maintenance costs, lowers the center of gravity and increases average speed, improves riding comfort, and may make possible lower fare to attract greater passenger traffic. It could be the answer to the need for improved service, and a passenger fare level competitive with that of buses.

If the "lightweight train" can achieve the 100 mile per hour of sustained speed expected of it, then it will definitely challenge the bus

The "Xplorer," which recently began service, is a lightweight, low-slung, articulated streamliner, carrying 392 coach passengers and patterned after the "Train X" concept. With a top speed of 120 m.p.h., it can take curves comfortably at higher speeds than can conventional trains.

and the automobile for the bulk of passenger traffic on inter-city runs. American highways are a long way from the time when motor travel at such speeds can be made with the necessary degree of safety. But even if the "lightweight train" does prove practicable in operation at such a speed, present passenger fare rates will still have to undergo a considerable drop to win passengers back from bus travel.

The Train of the Future

On hauls of 400 miles or less, the high-speed, lightweight train could also win back passengers from air travel. On a flight from New York to Boston, as much time is consumed in traveling from the center of the city to the airport and from the airport back downtown as is spent in actual flight. Since railroad termini are located in city centers, the passenger making the same New York–Boston trip would consume little if any more time in going from city to city.

Since the end of World War II, American railroads have spent more than one and a half billion dollars in the improvement of passenger facilities. Over fifteen thousand passenger trains are in daily operation,

hundreds of them boasting of the latest in equipment styling. The three outstanding developments in passenger service since the war include: installation of dome cars in 1945; increased utilization of the single-unit, self-propelled motor cars in 1950; and the beginnings of experimentation with the low-slung, lightweight cars in 1955–56.

The lightweight train is exactly what its name implies. Two 40-passenger cars of General Motors' Aero-Train weigh 32 tons as compared with the 65-ton weight of the standard railroad 80-passenger coach. As to the important factor of cost, such lightweight trains are expected to reduce train investment by 50 percent and maintenance and operating cost by nearly 60 percent. This is quite a saving. A stream-

lined train consisting of a two-unit Diesel locomotive, nine passenger cars, diner, mail and baggage car costs in the neighborhood of two and a half million dollars.

General Motors' Aero-Train has been in operation over the New York Central between Chicago and Detroit, and by the Pennsylvania Railroad between Pittsburgh and Philadelphia. The Talgo, made by American Car and Foundry Company, zips back and forth from Chicago and Peoria. Budd Company's Tubular Train is in operation between Washington and New York. Train X, or the Xplorer as it is called by the New York Central, speeds between Cleveland and Cincinnati.

The operation of these trains is being watched and checked from every point—efficiency, cost, and public response—by railroad management. It is much too early to tell whether they are the answer to the passenger traffic headache.

In the West, railroads are bidding for a return of passenger traffic with entirely different type trains. These are the high-level trains for the long hauls. The Santa Fe operates a double-decker train between Chi-

THE "JET ROCKET"

The "Jet Rocket" is one of the new, lightweight streamliners, introduced recently. Its guided car wheels and low center of gravity enable it to take curves at higher speeds than conventional trains. A special 1200-horsepower Diesel-electric locomotive powers the train.

cago and Los Angeles. This train was built for luxury and leg-comfort. Each upper-level coach seats from sixty-eight to seventy-two passengers. The bottom level is for baggage, lounges, and rest rooms. The dome car has become extremely popular with passengers in the mountainous and scenic areas. They provide a sweeping view of towering peaks, deep valleys, canyons, and splashing mountain falls. The addition of floodlights for the illumination of the passing countryside at night has increased the dome car's popularity. Some of these cars are equipped with speedometers—a feature of special interest to the younger traveler.

The Train of the Future

Railroads are continually experimenting with devices to make train travel not only more comfortable but more interesting. The Rock Island Railroad is experimenting with television to give passengers an "engineer's eye" view on a trip. On the Rock Island's low-slung streamliner between Chicago and Peoria, a television camera was installed just to the left of the center of the locomotive cab. A coaxial cable was strung back to a large-screen receiver located in the parlor car. Passengers could not only see what was passing on either side, but could get a view of what was coming at them straight ahead.

SIGHTSEERS PARADISE

Full-length dome car of the "Olympian Hiawatha" skirts the Wisconsin River as it passes Wisconsin Dells, Wisconsin.

Passenger comfort, faster trains, expanded facilities to make train trips more interesting are the major developments by railroads in their efforts to increase passenger traffic. They are not the only ones, though. Roadbeds are being improved. Rails of greater length, reducing the number of track joints, are being laid. These rails are of tougher, stronger steel. Other behind-the-scenes improvements include additional installation of electronic communication systems, radio, television, micro-wave, and induction circuits. These will help speed the trains over the better tracks, with fewer interruptions and with greater safety.

Railroads are making it easier for the passenger to purchase his ticket also. Electronic reservation bureaus are in service in many major centers. Installment purchasing of railroad tickets has been tried.

By constant experimentation, American railroads may solve their passenger traffic problem. The lightweight train may do it. The double-decker, vista-domed coach may do it. Additional services may help out. Only time will tell.

Time, though, will never erase the thrill which comes to the listener from the eerie wail of a train's whistle late at night, echoing against mountains, or bouncing across a plain. That whistle will forever be a clarion sounding the greatness of the American railroad and its contribution to the greatness of America.

CHAPTER XII

ROUNDHOUSE ROUNDUP

OF ALL the forms of transportation, from the stagecoach to the jet plane, probably none has been as widely written about, sung about, rhymed about, and joked about as the train. Railroad humor is of a special type, unlike that of any other industry.

Railroading has also developed a language of its own. If a *Big Ox* told the *Pig Mauler* the *highliner* was late, and he'd better have his *Diamond Cracker* give him plenty of *fog*, the translation would be, that the *conductor* told the *engineer* the *fast express* was late and the *fireman* had better build up plenty of *steam*. Or if you saw a *Baby Lifter* polishing his *brain plate*, you'd be watching a *passenger trainman* shining up his *badge*. A glossary is printed in the back of this book.

Some railroad humor has its grim overtones, particularly songs and poems about wrecks. The *Ballad of Casey Jones* is the classic example. Even today, jingles written about motorists trying to beat the train to the crossing are certainly more sombre than witty, such as:

A reckless man stepped on the gas
And tried a railway train to pass.
He reached the middle of the track,
And now he twangs a harp—alack!

Or:

The gates were down, but Simon Hay
Decided to his sorrow—
To speed across the right of way.
His funeral is tomorrow.

Pathos tinged with humor is to be found on the granite monument in Evergreen Cemetery, Colorado Springs, marking the grave of Charles B. Gunn, a railroad conductor who died in 1935. On the tombstone is the question:

Papa—Did you wind your watch?

It would not be too much of an exaggeration to state that there are as many stories, anecdotes, songs, and poems about railroads as there are miles of rails. Oddities, too, covering every topic from lost babies to the fact that no two of the ten thousand ticket punches used by railroad conductors make the same hole in the same shape, are sprinkled over every mile of roadbed.

One really amusing incident took place recently not in America but Czechoslovakia. When the conductor was collecting tickets, he found that every one of his passengers was on the wrong train. Or so it appeared, until one passenger suggested that the conductor might be on the wrong train. He was.

Lost valuables are always turning up on railroad cars. Once, a Pullman porter stripping a berth found a diamond ring worth $120,000. Another Pullman porter found a diamond necklace, a pearl necklace, a 14-diamond bar pin, a set of pearl earrings, and a platinum wrist watch, all tucked under a pillow, and worth $75,000.

Imagine the surprise of the Pullman porter when returning a batch of freshly-shined shoes to discover the aisle of his car strewn with hundred dollar bills! A cautious (?) traveler had carefully hidden the money in his shoes, then placed them outside his berth to be shined. The bills had dropped out an hour or so earlier when the porter had picked them up for shining.

In the gold-rush town of Deadwood, South Dakota, workmen discovered $1,200 in twenty-dollar bills when they dismantled an old railroad depot.

Of all articles left on trains, briefcases head the list, closely followed by wallets, watches, golf clubs, and even such strange things as canary birds and homing pigeons.

A smart trainman on a circus train was once faced with the problem of getting a giraffe under a low bridge. He solved his dilemma by drop-

ping a carrot on the car floor and moved the train under the bridge while the giraffe's head was down munching on the carrot.

In Alaska, railroads have moose trouble. The huge animals get on the track and sometimes run for miles just ahead of the train. If the engineer sounds his whistle, the moose are likely to turn around and do battle with the engine.

Conductor J. D. Hay of Washington, New Jersey, once went all out in providing a unique service for one of his passengers. A lady commuter told him that in her haste to catch the train, she forgot to turn off the electric iron and feared her house would catch on fire. A few minutes later, at the next station, Hay phoned back to the police, who drove to the lady's home and switched off her iron.

Any railroad man can sit up all night telling one story after another. Here are some most often told:

ENOUGH WAS ENOUGH

Cyrus H. Jenks was a division superintendent for the Great Northern at Crookston, Minnesota, when that railroad was a youngster. One day he received a telegram stating that a locomotive had fallen into the turntable pit at the Crookston roundhouse. A hand derrick, the wire went on, was being used to pull it out. At the next station, Jenks received another wire, telling him the hand derrick had fallen into the pit, and should a steam derrick now be tried? Jenks shot off this reply: "Leave steam derrick where it is. No more room in pit."

FALSE ECONOMY

James J. Hill, builder of the Great Northern, was a most thrifty man. On one of his inspection rounds he found a new track spike lying in the roadbed. Furious at such waste, he sought out the section foreman. The foreman knew Hill's temper. Before the boss could blast out at such shameful waste, the foreman spoke: "Thanks for finding that spike, Mr. Hill. I've had three men looking for it for nearly a week."

HE CAME BACK FOR MORE

They say this happened a while back in South Texas when the Southern Pacific's well-known streamliner, the *Sunset Limited,* was marooned

by a flood and its hundreds of passengers taken from the high water by boat and helicopter. A helicopter pilot, picking up a Mexican from the waterbound train, thought the face looked familiar. "Didn't I already rescue you today?" he asked. "Si, Senor," replied the Mexican, "but I enjoy so much riding in helicopter, I come back in rowboat."

IMPROVING THE BREED IN OKLAHOMA

The superintendent of a railroad in Oklahoma was discussing with his attorneys the large number of claims which farmers were filing against the company on account of cattle being struck and killed by railway trains. However worthless an animal may have been before the accident, each claim represented it as being of the best blood in Oklahoma.

"Do you know," exclaimed the superintendent, beating the desk with his fist for emphasis, "I have reached the conclusion that nothing in Oklahoma so improves the breed of livestock as crossing it with a locomotive."

INEXPLICABLE

The grizzled old mountaineer, paying his first visit to a railroad, was fascinated by the switch engine shuttling back and forth in the freight yard. Scratching his chin, he turned and remarked to his friend:

"I can understand how the engine pulls the cars. I've got that all figured out. But I'll be durned if I can see how the cars pull the engine back."

A RESOURCEFUL GOAT

There was a man named Joseph Dunn,
Who bought a billygoat just for fun.
One day the goat, prone to dine,
Ate a red shirt right off the line.

Then Dunn to the goat did say:
"Your time has come; you'll die today."
And took him to the railroad track,
And bound him there upon his back.

As the train approached with rush and roar,
Goat used his brain as ne'er before,
And with a mighty shriek of pain,
Coughed up the shirt and flagged the train.

Roundhouse Roundup

TRAIN STOPPED BY AN ANT

For no obvious reason, a crack passenger train speeding through Oklahoma recently was brought to a halt by a red semaphore signal. The "all clear" signal was received fifteen minutes later, and the train continued its run.

The stop was not scheduled or ordered by the dispatcher. Signalmen were dispatched to the vicinity to ascertain the cause. They found that a tiny ant had crawled into the delicate switch mechanism controlling the electric motor which operates the signal arm and set the red light that stopped the train. The ant did not survive to repeat its action.

A GENTLE DISPOSITION

Brady, the railroad superintendent, insisted on detailed reports on all livestock killed by trains on his division. A rule of the company required the section foreman to report all such accidents promptly. One day Brady received a report from section-foreman Pat Dugan that a cow was killed near Milepost 20 the day before. Details were meager. Brady wired Dugan: "Wire disposition of cow killed near Milepost 20." Dugan replied: "The disposition of the cow was very gentle."

HIGH ON THE HOG

A Mississippi farmer wrote the claim agent of a railroad as follows:

My razor-back roamed your track
A week ago today,
Your number nine came down the line
And snuffed his life away.

You can't blame me; the hog, you see,
Strolled through a cattle gate.
So kindly pen a check for ten,
This debt to liquidate.

The claim agent, being struck with the form of the letter, replied in kind:

Our Number Nine came down the line
And killed your hog, we know,
But razor-backs on railroad tracks
Quite often come to woe.
Therefore, my friend, we cannot send
The check for which you pine.
Just bury the dead, plant o'er his head,
"Here lies a foolish swine."

CURIOUS RAILROAD LAWS

Some states have laws pertaining to railroads that are most amusing. Many of them are old blue laws and while still on the statute books are not enforced.

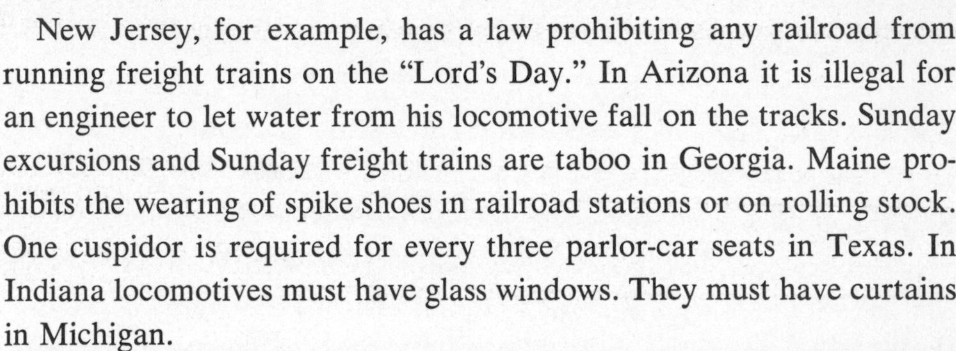

New Jersey, for example, has a law prohibiting any railroad from running freight trains on the "Lord's Day." In Arizona it is illegal for an engineer to let water from his locomotive fall on the tracks. Sunday excursions and Sunday freight trains are taboo in Georgia. Maine prohibits the wearing of spike shoes in railroad stations or on rolling stock. One cuspidor is required for every three parlor-car seats in Texas. In Indiana locomotives must have glass windows. They must have curtains in Michigan.

Nebraska has a law stating that any animal hit by a train must be given first aid and then taken to the humane society. In Minnesota, a conductor may be jailed for failure to arrest a gambler. Any passenger is required by law to assist the conductor in ejecting an unwanted passenger in Florida. It is against the law to sneeze on a train in West Virginia.

Just how could the provisions of this old Kansas law be observed? "When two trains are scheduled to meet at a railroad crossing within five minutes of each other, both trains must come to a halt and neither can start until the other is out of sight."

BONANZA

Patrick O'Toole had gotten a job as a brakeman on a railroad in a mountainous section of Pennsylvania, and was paid on the basis of miles run.

On one of the first trips, the engineer lost control of his train and it went speeding down the steep grades at a dangerous rate.

Suddenly the conductor saw his Irish companion, who had been clinging to the running-board for dear life, make a move as though to rise, and, fearful that he intended to jump, the conductor yelled: "Don't jump! You'll be killed!"

Pat shouted back: "Do you think I'm fool enough to jump when I'm makin' money as fast as I am now?"

A 300-MILE SLICE

A golf ball that O. P. Seeman, agent of the Canadian National at Port Colborne, Ontario, had sliced when driving from the ninth tee of the Port Colborne Country Club course traveled 300 miles and then came back to him. Mr. Seeman's tee shot not only went out of bounds but also disappeared into an open boxcar of a moving train. A few days later he received a package from Walkerville, Ontario, which contained the lost ball. The agent of the Canadian National at Walkerville had found the ball in the car and, recognizing the name of his fellow agent on it, had mailed it back to him.

SOME RAILROAD STATISTICS

To give the reader an idea of the size of the American railway system today, here are some enlightening statistics: The total rail line in the United States adds up to 220,300 miles. There are 31,419 locomotives, 31,800 passenger cars, and 1,700,300 freight cars in service. The average freight train is made up of 66.1 cars. In 1955 freight revenues amounted to $8,538,336,192 and passenger revenues added up to a total of $743,444,763.

The people who work for the railways of the United States number 1,058,216. Of these, 235,541 are employed as engineers, firemen, conductors, brakemen and other train and engine service men. An army of 273,155 men take care of maintaining equipment and stores, and there are 14,196 yardmasters, switchtenders and hostlers. There are also 196,000 men employed in the maintenance of way and structures, and 125,552 working as telegraphers, ticket agents, truckers, etc. Finally, there are over 200,000 white-collar workers—which include everyone from stenographer typists to company presidents—who make up the vast, intricate office organization. The 1955 payroll for all of these employees amounted to a staggering $4,993,662,226.

GLOSSARY OF RAILROAD SLANG

Reproduced by the courtesy of RAILROAD Magazine

age—Term of time in service, usually referring to Seniority.
air monkey—Air-brake repairman.
alley—Clear track.
anchor them—Set the brakes on still cars.
artist—A general term usually referring to some workman, particularly adept, and usually with such prefix as brake, pin, speed, etc.

baby lifter—Passenger brakeman.
bakehead—Locomotive fireman.
bath—Sometimes used in reference to taking water at a tank where the spout is short or not adjusted properly.
batting 'em out—Used generally by switchmen when goat (yard engine) has hold of a string of cars kicking them all over the yard.
battleship—Usually referred to the superheater type or any large locomotive.
beanery—A railroad eating house.
beanery queen—Waitress.
bee hive—Yard office.
bell bottom brakemen—College students.
bell ringer—Fireman.
bend the iron—Change the position of a switch.
bend the rust—Change the position of a switch.
big hole—Emergency position of the air-brake valve; the act of abruptly applying the brakes to the full reduction.
big hook—Wrecking crane.
big o—Freight conductor.
big ox—Conductor of either freight or passenger.
black diamonds—Company coal.
blow up—To quit a job suddenly.
board—A fixed signal regulating railroad traffic and usually referred to as a slow board, order board, clear board (for clear tracks) or red board (stop).
boiler header—Riding in cab.
boomer—The drifting type of railroad man who travels from road to road and stays but a very short time at any one place. The term was derived from the pioneer days of railroad booms along new frontiers and originally was applied to men who followed these boom camps.
brain plate—Trainman's badge.
brainless wonder—Conductor, engineer, fireman or any official who does queer things in the opinion of his fellows.
brains—Conductor.
brass collar—Applied to members of the official family.
brass hat—A term applicable to officials.
brass pounder—A telegraph operator.
brownies—Demerit marks placed against an employee's record.
brownie box—Superintendent's car.
buggy—Caboose; passenger car; boxcar.
bug torch—Trainman's lantern.
bull—Special agent or railroad police officer.
bullgine—Steam locomotive.
bumper—A post at end of spur track.

cage—Caboose.
caller—Employee whose duty it is to call out a train and engine crew.
calliope—Steam locomotive.
canned—To be taken out of service.
captain—A term applied to conductor, either passenger or freight.
car toad—Car repairer; there are many variations of this word viz: car knock, car tank, car whack, etc.
car whacker—Car repairman.
caser—Silver dollar.
century—Hundred-dollar bill.
chariot—Sometimes applied to passenger cars, but most frequently to cabooses.
chasing the red—The act of a flagman who has gone back with red flag or red light to protect a train.
cinder cruncher—A switchman.
cinder snapper—A passenger who rides the open platform on observation cars.
clown—A switchman or yard brakeman.
clown wagon—Caboose.
club—Hickory pole about three feet long found on some railroads and required by the management to be carried around by a trainman in addition to his raincoat and lantern.
club winder—Switchman or brakeman.
cornered—When a car, not in the clear on a siding, is struck by a passing train or engine.
corn field meet—Where two trains meet head-on, both trying to use the same main line.
cow cage—Stock car.
cow catcher—The pilot.
crib—Caboose.
cripple—A defective car or one that needs repairs.
croaker—Doctor.
crowning him—Coupling a caboose on a train when it is made up.
crummy—Caboose.
cupola—The observation tower on a caboose.
cushions—A term referring to passenger cars.
cut—A few cars attached to the goat or engine; several cars coupled together anywhere.

dancing on the carpet—Called to the superintendent's office for investigation or dicipline.
deadhead—Fireman's vernacular for brakeman; employee riding over the road on company pass and on company business.
deck—The floor part of a locomotive cab.
decorate—The act of riding on top of freight cars as required on mountains or passing stations on certain railroads.
detainer—Usually applied to the train dispatcher.
diamond—Crossover.
diamond cracker—Fireman.
dick—Railroad detective.
dinger—Yardmaster or assistant yardmaster.
dinky—Engine without tender used around roundhouse and backshop to do the switching.
dog catcher—A crew sent to relieve a crew that has become outlawed.
dog house—Caboose.
dolly—Applied to switch stand.
dope—Orders; official instructions.
drag—A heavy train of dead freight; any kind of train.
draw bar flagging—The act of a brakeman leaning up against the draw bar on the caboose to protect the rear end of his train.
drink—To take water for the locomotive.
drone cage—Private car.

drop—A switching movement.

drummer—Yard conductor.

duckets—Hat checks.

dynamiter—A car on which a defective air mechanism sends the brakes into full emergency when only service application is given from the engine.

eagle-eye—Locomotive engineer.

end man—The brakeman or rear brakeman, usually on freight trains.

family disturber—Pay car.

fireboy—Locomotive fireman.

first reader—Conductor's train book.

fist—Operator's handwriting.

flag—To work under an assumed name.

flat—A type of freight car.

flat wheel—A car wheel that has flat spots on the tread; also applied to an employee who walks lame or limps.

flimsy—Train Order.

floater—Same as a boomer.

flop—Bed.

flying switch—A switching movement.

fog—Steam.

foot-board—The step on the front end and rear end of switch and freight engines.

freeze hub—Cool a heated journal.

frog—An implement for rerailing wheels.

gandy dancer—Track laborer.

gangway—The space between the rear cab post of a locomotive and the tender.

garden—A freight yard.

gate—A switch.

general—Yardmaster.

glimmer—Switchman's lantern.

glory—String of empties; death by accident.

goat—A yard engine.

go high—The act of decorating or climbing to the top of box cars to receive signals or to transmit signals or to apply hand brakes.

g. m.—General Manager.

gon—A gondola or steel-sides, flat-bottom coal car.

grabber—Conductor.

gramaphone—Telephone.

graveyard watch—12:01 to 8:00 A.M.

greasy spoon—A railroad eating house.

green backs—Frogs for rerailing cars or engines.

gum shoe—Railroad policeman.

gun—A torpedo; the injector on the locomotive which forces water from tank to boiler.

hack—Another term for caboose.

ham—A telegraph operator. Usually referred to one of a poorer variety.

hand shoes—Gloves.

harness—Passenger conductor's uniform.

hay burner—Hand oil lantern.

head man—The brakeman who, on freight trains, rides the engine.

head pin—The head brakeman.

hearse—Caboose.

herder—A man who couples engines on and takes them off on the arrival and departure of trains.

highball—Signal waved by the hand or by lamp in a high, wide semiarc, the meaning of which is to get out of town at full speed ahead.

highball artist—A locomotive engineer who is noted for fast running.

high daddy—Make a flying switch; drop.

high iron—The main line or the high speed track of a system of main tracks.

highliner—Main line fast passenger.

high wheeler—Passenger locomotive; a fast passenger train; a highball artist.

hitting the grit—Falling off a car.

hog—A locomotive.

hogger—A locomotive engineer.

hoghead—A locomotive engineer.

hog law—The federal statute which provides that all train and engine crews tie up after sixteen hours of continuous service; also called the dog law.

hole—Term applied to passing track where one train pulls in to meet another.

home guard—One who stays with one railroad.

hook—Wrecking crane or auxiliary.

hopper—A steel-sided coal car with a hopper bottom which allows the unloading from that point.

hop-toad—Derail.

hose coupler—A brakeman who handles trains around a big passenger terminal with the road engine by himself.

hot box—Overheated journal or bearing.

hot footer—Engineer or conductor in switching service who is always in a hurry.

hot shot—A fast train of any class. Sometimes called a highball run.

housetracks—Tracks adjacent to or used in connection with a railroad-owned freight house, warehouse or similar facility, principally for handling and moving freight.

hump—An artificial knoll at the end of a classification yard over which cars are pushed to be allowed to roll to separate tracks on their own momentum.

hut—A term sometimes applied to a caboose and sometimes applied to the cab of a locomotive.

in the hole—On a siding.

investigation—Up on the carpet.

iron skull—A boiler maker.

jack—Locomotive.

jam buster—Assistant yardmaster.

jewel—Journal brass.

jerk soup or **jerk a drink**—To take water from a track pan without stopping the train.

jigger—A full tonnage train of dead freight.

johnson bar—Old reverse lever on a locomotive.

juggler—A term applied sometimes to members of the train crew of way freight runs, whose duties require them to load and unload less than carload freight at station stops.

kangaroo court—A hearing at which matters of main-line mix-ups are investigated and disposed of.

keeley—Water can for hot or heated journals.

kettle—A locomotive.

kick—Applied to switching; the act of pushing a car or cars at speed ahead or behind an engine, and then suddenly cutting the car or cars loose from the engine while the brakes are applied quickly to the engine, thus allowing the cars to be kicked free.

kicker—A triple valve that sticks and throws brakes into emergency with application of air and sometimes by a bump of the train.

king—Freight conductor—sometimes applied to the yardmaster.

king snipe—Foreman of track gang.

knowledge box—Yardmaster's office.

ladder—The main track of a system of tracks which comprise a yard and from which each individual track leads off - also called a lead.
lead—See ladder.
letters—Service certificates.
lever-jerker—Interlocker lever man.
lightning slinger—Telegraph operator.
lizard scorcher—Cook.
louse cage—Caboose.
lung—Drawbar.

main iron—Main track.
main pin—An official.
main stem—The main line.
making a hitch—Coupling two cars together.
mallet type locomotive—Used for heavy freight hauling, and to help heavy trains up steep grades.
manifest—Fast freight, usually made up of merchandise and perishables.
marker—Rear end signal.
master—Conductor.
master maniac—The master mechanic.
master mind—Sometimes applied to trainmaster, yardmaster and conductor, also to the train dispatcher.
meal book—Pie card or grazing ticket.
mill—Steam locomotive; typewriter.
mill kettle—Locomotive.
modoc—Employees' train.
monkey house—Caboose.
monkey motion—Link motion.
mud chicken—Surveyor.
mudhop—Yard clerk.

no-bill—A loaded car for which there is no waybill; non-union employee.
non-air—A non-union railroad worker.
number dummy—Yard clerk.
number grabber—Car clerk.
nut splitter—Machinist.

old man—Superintendent.
op—A telegraph operator.
o.r.c.—A conductor.
order board—A fixed signal to indicate to approaching trains whether to pick up train orders or to proceed.
ornament—Station Master.
o-sing—Reporting a train by a station to the division dispatcher.
outlawed—A crew that has worked 16 hours, the limit allowed by law.

paddle—Semaphore signal.
palace—A term applied to the caboose.
parlor—Caboose.
parlor man—The hind brakeman or flagman on a freight train.
pie card—A card issued by a railroad to employees entitling them to meals.
pig—Locomotive.
pig mauler—Locomotive engineer.
pig pen—Locomotive roundhouse.
pin—Sometimes applied to a brakeman.
pin ahead and pick up two behind one—Cut off the engine and pick up three cars from the siding, put two on the train and set the first one back on the siding.
pin for home—To go home.
pinhead—Applied to brakeman.
pink—Caution card.
pinner—Switchman that follows.
pin-puller—The man who cuts off the cars switching.
play ball—Get busy; go to work; quit fooling.
plug—One horse passenger train.
possum belly—Tool box under caboose.
pull the pin—To resign, or quit a job.
putty—Steam.

rail—A railroad employee. Usually referred to men in transportation service.
rattler—A freight train.
rawhider—A conductor or engineer who is especially hard on men and equipment. This term is chiefly applied to engineers who punish locomotives to the limit without getting satisfactory results.
red ball—Fast freight.
red board—Fixed signal to stop.
red onion—Railroad eating house.
reefer—Refrigerator car.
ringmaster—Yardmaster.
roof garden—A mallet type or a helper on a mountain job.
rubberneck—Observation car.
rule g—Thou shalt not drink.
runty—dwarf signal.

sacred ox—A mallet type or a helper on a mountain job.
scissor-bill—Applied to either yard or road brakeman and a term which is not considered complimentary; a student in train service.
scoop—The step on the front and rear-end of switch engines.
secret works—Automatic air-brake application.
shack—A brakeman.
shack stinger—Brakeman.
shanty—A caboose.
shining time—Starting time.
shuffle the deck—Used by local brakemen for switching housetracks at every station.
shunting boiler—Switch engine.
sidedoor pullman—Boxcar.
skipper—Conductor.
slave driver—Yardmaster.
smart alec—Conductor.
smoke—Fireman.
smoker—Locomotive.
smoking 'em—A method of getting from one station to another without orders, moving along slowly, watching for smoke of an approaching train. Very dangerous business but often done.
snake—Switchman.
snipe—Track laborer.
snoozer—Pullman car.
soft bellies—Wooden frame cars.
spar—A pole used to shove cars in the clear when switching.
speedy—Call boy.
spotter—A man assigned to snoop around to check up on conduct of employees.
stick—A staff used on certain stretches of track for the purpose of controlling the block. It is carried by engine crews from one station to another.
stinger—Brakeman.
stoker—Fireman.
stopper puller—A member of the crew that follows the engine in switching.
string—A cut of cars; several cars coupled together.
strings—Telegraph wires.
student—A learner in either telegraph, train or engine service.
super—A superintendent.
swell head—Conductor.

tallowpot—Locomotive fireman.
tank—Locomotive tender.
teakettle—Usually applied to leaky old locomotives.
teddy—Sixteen-hour law.
the hook—The wrecker.
thousand miler—A starched blue shirt with an attachable starched blue collar of deep hue worn by railroad men universally and especially as an insignia of rank among boomers of a bygone era.
ticket punch—Pair of pliers.
tie 'em down—To set hand brakes.
toad—Derailer.
toepath—Running board.
train detainer—Train dispatcher.
train line—The pipe that carries the compressed air used to operate the air brakes.
traveling grunt—A road foreman of engines.
traveling man—Usually applied to the traveling engineer or the traveling fireman.
trick—Applied to tour of duty.
trip—The course of a tour of duty from one terminal to another and return.

underground hog—Chief engineer.

varnished wagons—Passenger train equipment.

wagons—See buggy.
washout—A stop signal waved violently by using both arms and swinging them in a downward arc by day, and swinging a lamp in a wide, low semicircle across the tracks by night.
way-car—Caboose.
shale belly—A type of coal car.
when do you shine?—What time were you called for.
willie—Waybill.
wing her—Set the brakes on a moving train.
wye—Tracks running off main line or lead, forming rough letter "Y" and used to turn cars or to reverse direction of trains. Used to reverse engines at points where no turntable is available.

yard—A system of tracks for the making of trains or the storing of cars. A system of tracks surrounded by a high board fence run and inhabited by a bunch of natives (regular employees) that will not let a train in or out.—Boomer's version.
y.m.—Yardmaster.

zulu—An emigrant outfit.

RAILROAD WHISTLE TALK

Train whistles, too, have their own language. Every toot and series of toots has a special meaning. Here they are, a dot meaning a short toot, a dash meaning a long toot:

• Apply brakes. Stop.
–– Release brakes. Proceed.
–••• Flagman go back and protect rear of train.
–––– Flagman return from west or south.
––––– Flagman return from east or north.
•••– Protect front of train.
•• Answer to any signal not otherwise provided for.
••• When standing, to back up. When running, to stop at next passenger station.
•••• Call for signals.
––•– Approaching highway crossing at grade.
— Approaching stations, junctions and railroad crossings.
••– Approaching meeting, or waiting, points of trains.
A number of short toots is an alarm for persons or livestock on the track.

HISTORICAL HIGHLIGHTS OF AMERICAN RAILROADS

In 1807, Silas Whitney operated a horse-drawn and gravity wooden tramway on Beacon Hill in Boston. This marked the beginning of vehicles operating on tracks in the United States. Since then, almost every year has seen an outstanding event in the further development of America's great railroad system. The following is a chronology of some of the most outstanding of those dates.

February 6, 1815—John Stevens, of Hoboken, was granted first railroad charter in America by the New Jersey Legislature.

February 9, 1825—First locomotive to run on rails in America, built by John Stevens and operated experimentally on a half-mile circular track at Hoboken, N.J.

October 7, 1826—Gridley Bryant's Granite Railway was opened at Quincy, Mass., to transport granite used in building Bunker Hill Monument; horses supplied motive power.

August 8, 1829—Locomotive *Stourbridge Lion,* imported from England, put on track at Honesdale, Pa., and operated three miles with Horatio Allen as engineer.

August 25, 1830—Trial trip of Peter Cooper's locomotive *Tom Thumb,* from Baltimore to Ellicott's Mills, Md., and return.

December 25, 1830—Railroad at Charleston, S. C., began scheduled passenger service, using American-built locomotive, *Best Friend of Charleston;* the first public carrier by rail in South Carolina and the first railroad in America to use steam power in regular service; completed to Hamburg, S. C., 136 miles, on October 3, 1833.

August 9, 1831—First steam train in New York State ran from Albany to Schenectady, pulled by locomotive *DeWitt Clinton.*

November, 1831—United States Mails carried for first time by rail—in South Carolina.

1831—A pine-knot fire on open-platform car in South Carolina served as first locomotive headlight.

November 23, 1832—*Old Ironsides,* Matthias Baldwin's first locomotive, made initial run from Philadelphia toward Germantown.

June 6, 1833—Andrew Jackson became the first President of the United States to ride on a railroad train—between Ellicott's Mills, Md., and Baltimore.

August 25, 1835—First railroad to Washington, D. C., opened from Baltimore.

1836—First two locomotives known to have been equipped with whistles were built at Lowell, Mass., under the supervision of George Washington Whistler. The *Hicksville* was put in service at Jamaica, Long Island, and was reported to make "a shrill, wild unearthly sound something like drawing a saw flat across a bar of iron."

1837—World's first sleeping car operated between Harrisburg and Chambersburg, Pa.—a remodeled day coach, crudely built.

January, 1838—New York (South Amboy) and Washington, D. C., linked by a chain of railroads.

March 4, 1839—America's first long-distance railway-express service started by William F. Harnden, former railroad conductor, between Boston and New York.

November 24, 1842—Rail route from Boston to Great Lakes at Buffalo completed.

1850—Oil lamps were introduced on trains for night travel; gas light in 1860; Pintsch gas in 1883; electricity in 1885; fluorescent lights in 1938.

September 22, 1851—First recorded use of telegraph for train dispatching took place at Turner (now Harriman), N. Y.

December 9, 1852—First locomotive west of Mississippi River, *The Pacific,* ran from St. Louis to Cheltenham, 5 miles.

December 24, 1852—Railroad from Baltimore completed to Ohio River at Wheeling.

January 24, 1853—All-rail route completed between Eastern cities and Chicago; several changes of cars were necessary, though.

1854—Luxurious, adjustable reclining-seat coaches, "night seats" as they were called, placed in service between Philadelphia and Baltimore.

February, 1855—Susan Morningstar, of Baltimore, Md., is recorded as the first woman railroad employee.

February 22, 1856—California's first railroad opened, Sacramento to Folsom.

September 27, 1856—World's longest railroad completed, Chicago to Cairo and Centralia to East Dubuque, 705½ miles.

September 1, 1859—First Pullman sleeping car left Bloomington, Ill., on overnight trip to Chicago; first Pullman conductor was Jonathan L. Barnes.

1860—Chicago, with eleven railroads, had become America's leading railway center.

April 12, 1862—Race and battle between Union soldiers on locomotive *General* and Confederates on locomotive *Texas,* from Big Shanty to Ringgold, between Atlanta and Chattanooga.

July 1, 1862—President Lincoln signed Act authorizing construction of a line of railroads from the Missouri River to the Pacific Coast.

1863—Dining cars introduced; ran between Philadelphia and Baltimore.

November 1, 1865—A tank car especially built for transporting oil took on its initial load at Titusville, Pa.

1866—Automatic block signals introduced.

1868—First Pullman-built dining car, the *Delmonico,* placed in service.

January 23, 1869—George Westinghouse applied for air-brake patent.

May 10, 1869—Golden Spike ceremony at Promontory, Utah, signalized completion of the first transcontinental rail route.

March 8, 1881—Completion of first rail route to Southern California via New Mexico and Arizona.

1881—Railway mileage in United States exceeded 100,000 route miles for the first time.

1881—Steam-heating system first installed in passenger trains, replacing stoves and hot-water heaters.

January 12, 1883—Completion of direct rail route from California to New Orleans; first through-train service began on February 5.

September 8, 1883—Entrance of first rail route from Great Lakes into Washington Territory celebrated.

November 25, 1884—Middle transcontinental route from Chicago to

Pacific Northwest joined at Huntington, Ore.; through traffic commenced December 1, 1884.

1886—Standardization of gauge (4 ft. 8½ in.) of railroads in the South completed, enabling interchange of cars throughout the country for first time.

June 17–18, 1887—Successful test runs were made of a passenger train hauled by an oil-burning locomotive, Altoona to Pittsburgh and return.

1887—First trains in America to be fully equipped with electric lights ran between New York and Chicago, Boston and New York, New York and Florida, and from Springfield, Mass., to Northampton.

January 6, 1893—Second rail route completed from Great Lakes to Puget Sound.

May 10, 1893—Locomotive No. "999" made the world's first 100-mile-an-hour record run.

1902—Railroad route mileage in United States passed the 200,000 mile mark.

June 12, 1905—Fastest train speed officially recorded on an American railroad was made on a 3-mile run near Ada, O., at 127.06 miles per hour.

May 19, 1909—Third northern rail route from Great Lakes to Puget Sound completed.

October 20, 1925—First Diesel-electric locomotive (a switcher) installed in railroad service.

1927—Beginning of modern developments in mechanical air-conditioning of railway passenger cars.

January 12, 1929—Cascade Tunnel, 7.79 miles in length, longest in Western Hemisphere, opened in Washington State.

May 24, 1931—World's first completely air-conditioned passenger train placed in service between Washington and New York.

May 26, 1934—First Diesel-electric powered streamlined train, completed April 9, 1934, ran non-stop 1,015 miles, Denver to Chicago, at an average speed of 77.6 miles per hour.

October 22–25, 1934—Diesel-powered streamlined train ran from Los Angeles to New York City, 3,258 miles, in 56 hours, 55 minutes; average over-all speed 57.2 miles per hour.

March, 1937—Two-way train telephone communication system inaugurated in mainline operations, between Albion, Pa., and North Bessemer Yard, Pittsburgh.

June 15, 1938—First 16-hour passenger train schedules put into effect between New York and Chicago.

July 23, 1945—First modern domed observation car introduced, operating between Chicago and Minneapolis.

September 2, 1945—V-J Day ended World War II; during 45 months of war, the railroads moved 90 percent of all Army and Navy freight and more than 97 percent of all military personnel in organized groups within the United States; the latter included the operation of 113,891 special troop trains.

May, 1952—Diesel ownership, as expressed in power units, exceeded ownership of steam locomotives for the first time—19,082 Diesel-electric units to 18,489 steam locomotives.

1956—Introduction of experimental low-slung, lightweight passenger trains.

January 1, 1957—More than 11 billion dollars spent for improvement of facilities and equipment since the end of World War II.

SELECTED LIST OF BOOKS ABOUT RAILROADS

Beebe, Lucius, *Highball*, D. Appleton-Century, 1945.

Beebe, Lucius and Charles Clegg, *Hear the Train Blow!*, E. P. Dutton & Co., 1952.

Botkin, B. A. and Harlow, A. F., *A Treasury of Railroad Folklore*, Crown Publishers, 1953.

Bowman, Hank W., *Pioneer Railroads*, Arco Publishing Co., 1954.

Downey, Fairfax, *Trail of the Iron Horse*, Charles Scribner's Sons, 1951.

Farrington, S. Kip, Jr., *Railroads at War*, Coward-McCann, 1944.

Henry, Robert Selph, *Trains*, Bobbs-Merrill Co., 1934.

———, *This Fascinating Railroad Business*, Bobbs-Merrill Co., 1946.

Holbrook, Stewart H., *The Age of the Moguls*, Doubleday, 1953.

———, *The Story of the American Railroads*, Crown Publishers, 1947.

———, *James J. Hill*, Alfred A. Knopf, 1955.

Hubbard, Freman H., *Railroad Avenue*, Whittlesey House, McGraw-Hill, 1945.

Morse, Frank P., *Cavalcade of the Rails*, E. P. Dutton, 1940.

O'Connell, John, *Railroad Album*, Popular Mechanics Press, 1954.

Rawson, Marion Nicholl, *From Here to Yender*, E. P. Dutton & Co., 1932.

Stevers, Martin D., *Steel Trails*, Grosset & Dunlap, 1933.

Throm, Edward L., *Popular Mechanics' Picture History of American Transportation*, Simon and Schuster, 1952.

NOTE: A complete bibliography of railroad literature would include thousands of books, bulletins, and reports. The Association of American Railroads, Washington 6, D. C., has compiled a list containing many books on this subject.

THE GROWTH OF AMERICAN RAILROADS

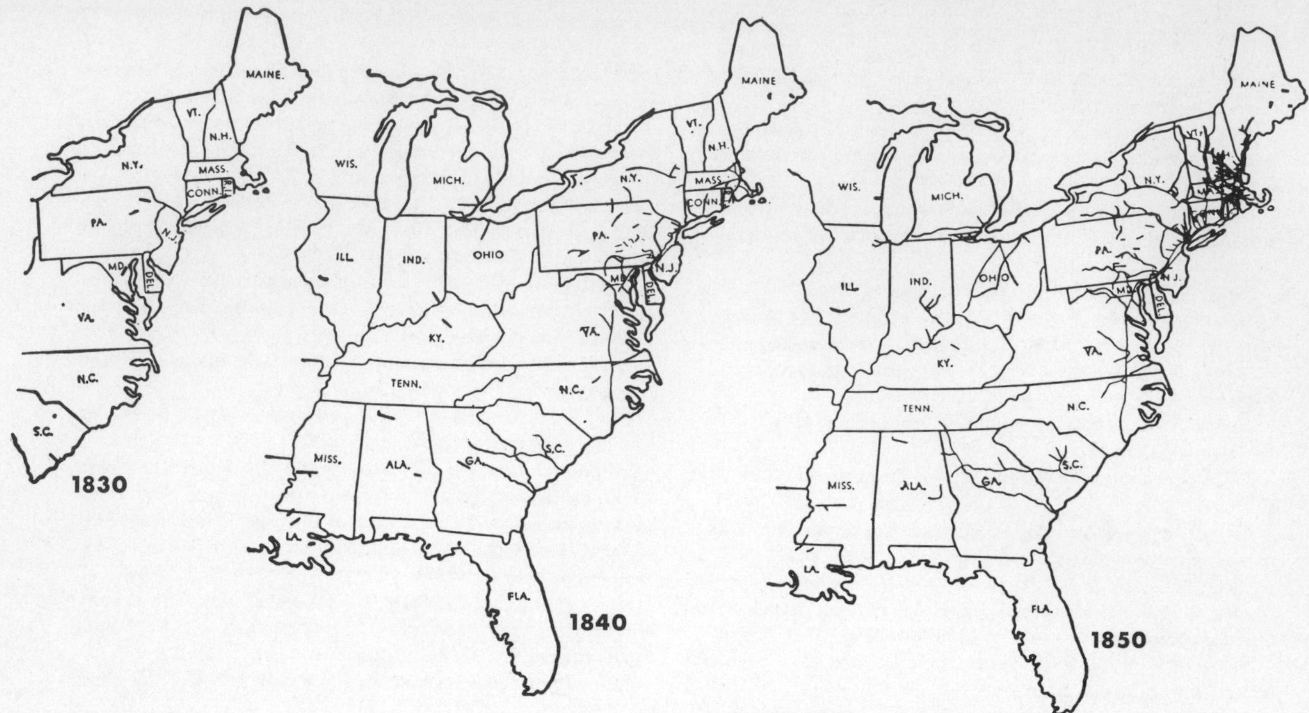

The early stages of railway development in America are shown by this set of maps. During the decade 1830-1840, the total length of completed railroad lines increased from 23 to 2,808 miles, and during the next ten years, more than 6,200 miles of railroad were opened, bringing the total network up to 9,021 miles in 1850. The most intensive growth during this period was in the Atlantic Seaboard states. In 1850, a trip from Boston or New York to Chicago was made by rail and lake steamers or by stagecoaches, and required several days. One could travel all the way from Boston to Wilmington, North Carolina, by rail, with several changes of cars and a few ferry trips en route. During the first twenty years of railway development, covered by these maps, the population of the United States nearly doubled.

1860 This map shows the extent of railway development just prior to the Civil War. The decade 1850-1860 was a period of rapid railway expansion, characterized by the extension of many short, disjointed lines into important rail routes. This decade marked the beginning of railway development in the region west of the Mississippi River. By 1860, the "Iron Horse" had penetrated westward to the Missouri River and was beginning to make itself felt in Iowa, Arkansas, Texas, and California.

1870 Although the War Between the States temporarily halted railway development, many projects were resumed or initiated soon after the close of that conflict. The nation's network increased from 30,626 miles in 1860 to 52,922 miles in 1870. An outstanding development of the decade was the construction of the first railroad to the Pacific Ocean, making it possible for the first time to travel all the way across the country by rail. Railway development in the Mississippi and Missouri valleys was especially notable during this period.

1890 The period from 1880 to 1890 was one of rapid expansion. More than 70,300 miles of new lines were opened in that decade, bringing the total network up to 163,597 miles. By 1890, several trunk line railroads extended to the Pacific. In thirty years from 1860 to 1890, the total mileage of the region west of the Mississippi River increased from 2,175 to 72,389, and the population of that area increased fourfold.

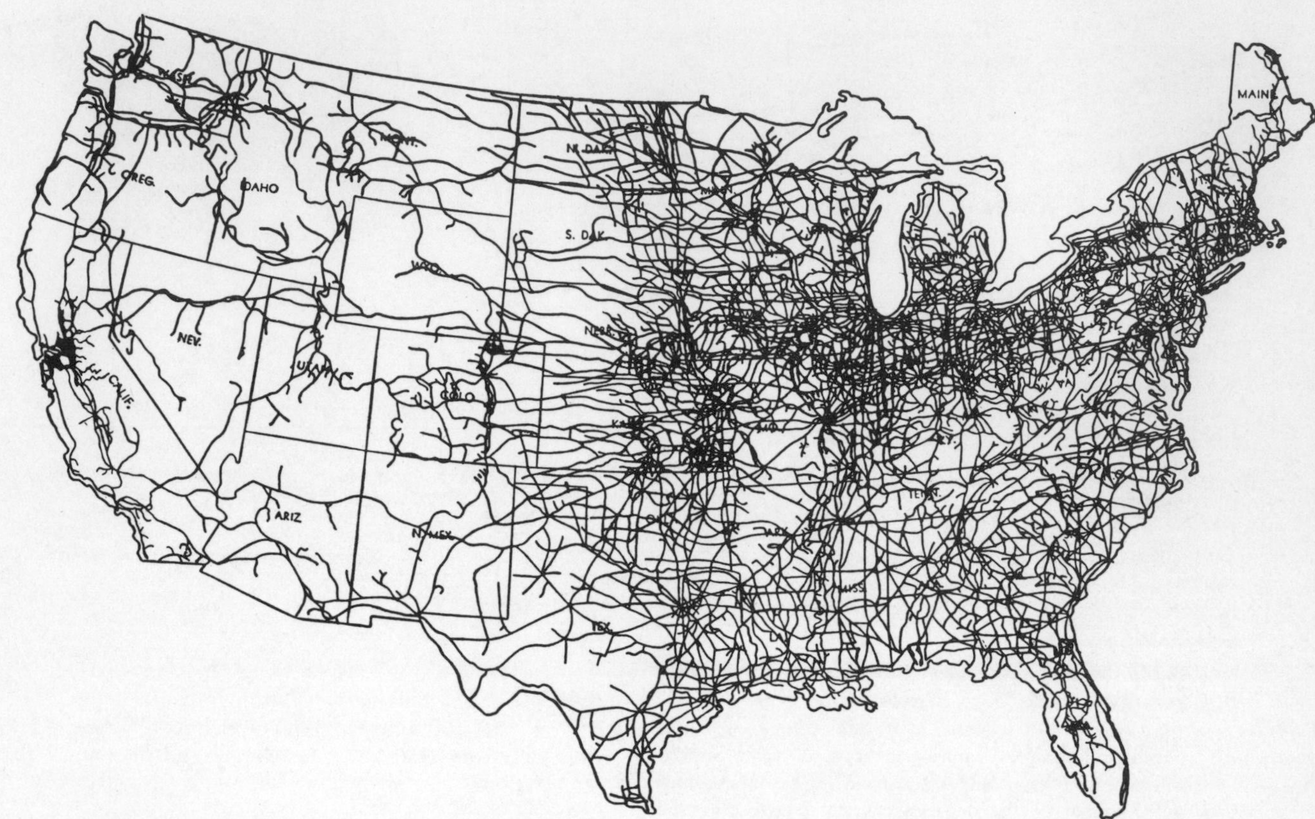

1956 Today, the American railroads embrace 221,000 miles of road and 393,000 miles of tracks. These railroads handle approximately 38 per cent of the commercial passenger and 51 per cent of the freight business of the nation, carry about 85 per cent of the United States mail and perform nearly all of the commercial express traffic of the nation. During World War II these railroads handled more than 90 per cent of the war freight and 97 per cent of the organized troop movements.

INDEX

(NOTE: Italicized page numbers refer to illustrations or their captions only.)